twitter

Tips, Tricks, and
Tweets

twitter

Tips, Tricks, and

Tweets

Paul McFedries

WILEY

Wiley Publishing, Inc.

Twitter Tips, Tricks, and Tweets

Published by
Wiley Publishing, Inc.
10475 Crosspoint Blvd.
Indianapolis, IN 46256
www.wiley.com

For general information on our other products and services or to obtain technical support, please contact our Customer Care Department within the U.S. at (877) 762-2974, outside the U.S. at (317) 572-3993 or fax (317) 572-4002.

Wiley also publishes its books in a variety of electronic formats. Some content that appears in print may not be available in electronic books.

Library of Congress Control Number: 2009925744

WILEY

About the Author

Paul McFedries is a technical writer who has been authoring computer books since 1991. He has more than 60 books to his credit, which together have sold more than three million copies worldwide. His current titles include the Wiley books *MySpace Visual Quick Tips*, *Internet Simplified*, *iPhone 3G Portable Genius*, *Teach Yourself VISUALLY Macs*, and *Teach Yourself VISUALLY Windows Vista*. Paul is also the proprietor of Word Spy, a Web site devoted to new words and phrases (see www.wordspy.com). Paul lives in Toronto with his wonderful wife, Karen, and their silly dog, Gypsy. Please visit Paul's personal Web site at www.mcfedries.com, or follow him on Twitter using his Twitter accounts @paulmcf, @wordspy, and @citizencoin.

Credits

Executive Editor
Jody Lefevere

Technical Editor
Jim Lefevere
www.jimlefevere.com

Copy Editor
Kim Heusel

Editorial Director
Robyn Siesky

Editorial Manager
Cricket Krengel

Vice President and Group Executive Publisher
Richard Swadley

Vice President and Executive Publisher
Barry Pruett

Business Manager
Amy Knies

Senior Marketing Manager
Sandy Smith

Project Coordinator
Kristie Rees

Graphics and Production Specialists
Ana Carrillo
Jennifer Henry
Andrea Hornberger
Clint Lahnen
Ron Terry

Quality Control Technician
Jessica Kramer

Proofreading
Penny L. Stuart

Indexing
Johnna VanHoose Dinse

To Karen, who follows my offline tweets.

Acknowledgments

Many writers believe that the essence of good writing is rewriting. Not me. I believe that the essence of good writing is good editing. I don't care how talented you are as a writer and how many times you rewrite each sentence, a good editor makes your writing better, period. Of course, there's a lot riding on that little word "good." Fortunately, the editorial team at Wiley is one of the best in the business, and I had the distinct pleasure of working with Cricket Krengel, Wiley's editorial manager, who easily qualifies as a great editor. Cricket: a thousand, nay a million thank-yous for bringing this book up to a level beyond its author. As you read this book, you'll notice that every i is dotted and every t is crossed, and for that I extend heartfelt thanks to this book's copy editor, the sharp-eyed Kim Heusel. Technical writing must be technically accurate, of course, or there's just no point to it. So for the often thankless tasking of taking all my techniques for a test drive, I thank this book's technical editor, Jim Lefevere. Finally, I would be remiss if I didn't also shout "Thank you!" at the top of my lungs to this book's acquisitions editor, Jody Lefevere, for asking me to write the book. I can't tell you how much fun I had writing it.

foreword

Social media is a phenomenon that's turning everyone into a publisher and distributor of media: from YouTube videos to blog posts to Twitter messages and even comments on the articles we read around the web, we're all becoming content creators. As the CEO and founder of Mashable.com, an online guide to social media, I've seen this trend evolve from the clunky old blogging software of years ago — for which you needed to understand web hosting and basic programming to even get started — to the effortless simplicity of a 140-character Twitter message (or Tweet).

Twitter is perhaps the simplest and most addictive social media tool of them all, and its unprecedented success has been both unexpected and inspirational. I've been fortunate to be part of that journey, tracking Twitter's growth on behalf of Mashable and posting updates about Twitter and social media to the @mashable Twitter account.

As you'll learn in this book, once the basic principles of Twitter are understood, the possibilities are almost limitless. In fact, much of the service's appeal comes from its simplicity: write anything you wish in 140-characters or less, and then share it with the world. Is it a chat room? Is it a way to send text messages to a group of friends? Is it a new technology for reading news headlines? Is it the world's simplest social network, a barebones version of MySpace and Facebook? It's all of those things and more: Twitter is whatever you make it.

Twitter is only three years old, but the service has been put to some inspirational, innovative and quirky uses already. Surgeons have Tweeted live from the operating room. A worldwide fundraising event was organized, garnering more than $250,000 for charity. More than one marriage proposal has been made (and accepted!). A British man traveled around the world to New Zealand, getting by thanks to the kindness of Twitter users. And in thousands of cities, Twitter fans have come together in real life Tweetups, making their virtual connections real.

Twitter's users are exceptionally inventive and resourceful, too. An expectant father created a device for his pregnant wife to wear: it sends a Twitter message every time their baby kicks. A software developer created a system that turns the lights on or off in his home by sending out a Tweet. You can even buy a kit for your plants that posts a Tweet when they need watering; a similar kit allows you to track your power consumption via Twitter.

Tweeting plants aren't the only non-human Twitter members. Both the Space Shuttle Endeavour and Mars Phoenix Lander posted Tweets during their missions for NASA, while London's Tower Bridge posts a Tweet when it opens or closes. There are Tweets from a whale on the ceiling of the Natural History Museum in New York City. And one of Twitter's most popular users is a cat in Waltham, Massachusetts.

All this innovation and creativity is part of Twitter's culture, it seems: a wealth of Tweet-powered services have sprung up, creating a flourishing ecosystem of so-called Twitter applications. There are tools to find Twitter users near you; Web sites that list the funniest Tweets (or the most insightful); services that rank Twitter users by their influence; and three-dimensional maps that show Tweets being posted around the world, every minute of the day.

More remarkable than all of these developments, however, is Twitter's profound effect on society: from news coverage to politics to customer relations and the nature of celebrity, this seemingly simple service is transforming entire industries.

Newspapers use Twitter as both a source of stories and a way to distribute their own headlines. Many of the top Twitter users are news agencies, and Twitter members have been known to Tweet about breaking news hours before its coverage on television. The effect on the media has been so dramatic; in fact, that one UK newspaper posted an April's Fool's joke claiming that it would cease publication of the paper and publish stories solely in Tweeted form.

News and politics go hand in hand, and politicians are equally cognizant of Twitter's power: US President Barack Obama has an enormous Twitter following, and his team posts occasional updates that request feedback from the American public. Obama is the most prominent among hundreds of Twittering politicians from numerous countries and political persuasions; of course, Twitter is non-partisan and international in its scope.

If Twitter can influence our political opinions, could it also determine what we buy? Some of the world's biggest brands hope so, and many have jumped into Twitterland with both feet. Some use the service for product announcements, while others post responses to questions and complaints from customers; some even host contests to win free products and services.

What about personal branding and celebrity? From Hollywood stars to sporting heroes to the world's most famous musicians, Twitter provides a connection between celebrities and their fans that is more direct than ever before. Some of the world's most recognizable names are using Twitter, giving us unprecedented insights into their everyday lives.

That's just a sampling of what you'll find on Twitter; it's inspiration, information, news, gossip, humor and remarkable personal stories. Twitter is all that we are, from our most exalted moments to our most mundane — and everything in between.

~ Pete Cashmore, CEO and founder of Mashable.com

contents

Chapter 4: How Do I Follow Other Twitter Users?. 48

introduction

What are you doing?

With that humble, even mundane, question, a company, a network, and a phenomenon were born.

What are you doing?

It's a question that seems crafted to elicit nothing but the most trivial of replies: I just woke up; I'm having bacon and eggs for breakfast; I'm in a boring meeting; I just finished dinner; I'm going to bed.

But a funny thing has happened in the three years or so that Twitter has been part of the social networking scene: Twitter users took the original What are you doing? question and morphed it into something more along the lines of What's happening now? That seemingly subtle change has made all the difference because it opens up a world of new questions: What are you reading? What great idea did you just come up with? What are you worried about? What interesting person did you just see or hear? What great information did you stumble upon on the Web? What hilarious video would you like to share?

Yes, you can still tell people what you're doing, and lots of Twitter users do just that. What's different now is that you're free to turn your Twitter experience into anything you want it to be. To do that, however, you need a guide to the ins and outs of Twitter and the tools, services, and sites that have sprung up in its wake. That's what *Twitter Tips, Tricks, and Tweets* aims to be. This book not only tells you everything you need to know to get started with Twitter and perform all of its standard chores, but it goes beyond the basics to show you how to wring every last bit of usefulness, education, and fun out of Twitter.

Who should read this book? You!

Some books are aimed squarely at specific types of people: beginners, programmers, left-handers, or whatever. Not this book:

- If you've never even heard of Twitter until this second, you can safely use this book to get started and see what all the fuss is about.

- If you've used Twitter for a while but haven't explored much, this book will be the map that shows you how to get to Twitter's useful and fun features and tools.

- If you already know your way around Twitter, I'm confident that this book will tell you a few things you don't know and will introduce you to some techniques you haven't yet tried.

- If you hate Twitter or are simply mystified by the whole thing, I hope this book will show you that although Twitter isn't the life-changing event that some folks make it out to be, it is useful and entertaining if you use it in a way that suits you.

The changing Twitter Web site

As I was writing this book, the Twitter programmers and designers were busy working on a revised version of the Twitter Web site. To help them get this new site tested and ready for prime time, they've been rolling it out to a few accounts to see what happens. This means there's a chance that the Twitter Web site you see when you create an account just might look a bit different than the version of the site that's featured in this book. Not to worry, though: all the techniques that I describe in this book still work in the new interface, so you won't get thrown for any loops.

That's all for now. I hope you enjoy the book.

Happy Twittering!

How Do I Get Started with Twitter?

1 2 3 4 5 6 7 8 9

Are you ready to share with the world select bits and pieces of your life, 140 characters (or less) at a time? I suspected as much. This means that you're ready to get started with Twitter, the microblogging service that's taking the online world by storm. In this chapter you begin, appropriately enough, at the beginning by learning how to set up and sign in to a Twitter account. Even if you've already got a Twitter account up and running, this chapter also takes you through a few other crucial Twitter techniques, including changing and resetting your Twitter password.

Setting Up Your Very Own Twitter Account

If all you want out of Twitter is to read a particular Twitterer's updates, then you don't need to bother creating your own account. Instead, point your favorite Web browser to http://twitter.com/*user*, where *user* is the person's user name on Twitter, and then peruse the updates that appear on the page.

This, of course, is no fun whatsoever. Twitter is all about sharing and participating in a community of fellow Twitterheads, and you can't do either of those things if you're sitting on the sidelines. Even better, joining Twitter literally takes only seconds of your time. So, without further ado (not that there's been much ado so far), here's how to join Twitter:

1. **Display Twitter's Create an Account page by navigating your Web browser to http://twitter.com/signup.** If you're already on http://twitter.com, click Get Started—Join!; if you're already viewing a Twitterer's updates, click Join Today!.

2. **Use the Full name text box to type the name that you want other people to see when they look at your Twitter profile.** Two things to consider here:

   - If you want people to find you on Twitter, be sure to type both your first and last names.
   - You can't include the text *twitter* anywhere in the name.
   - The maximum number of characters you can type is 20.

3. **In the Username text box, type the username you want to use on Twitter.** Here are some notes to bear in mind:

   - The username defines your Twitter address (it's http://twitter.com/*username*), it appears before each of your updates, and it appears in various other places in the Twitter landscape, so pick something you like and that has meaning.

 Don't sweat the username choice too much because you can always change it later.

   - The maximum number of characters is 15.
   - You can include any combination of letters, numbers, and underscores (_). All other characters are illegal (you can't even type them in the text box).
   - You can't include the text *twitter* anywhere in the username.
   - As you type, Twitter checks to see if your username is available. If you see "username has already been taken," then you're out of luck and need to try again. If you see "ok." then you're good to go.

4. **Use the Password text box to type a password for your Twitter account.** More informational notes:

- The password must be at least six characters long.

- As you type the password, Twitter rates the password strength: Weak, Good, Strong, or Very Strong. To get your password up to the Very Strong rating, make the password at least eight characters long, and include at least one number and one non-alphanumeric symbol.

5. **In the Email text box, type the e-mail address you want to use to receive Twitter notifications and other messages.** You learn in Chapter 2 how to customize these notifications. If you want to receive the Twitter newsletter, be sure to select the I want the inside scoop check box.

6. **Use the Type the words above field to type the two words you see in the captcha box.** Figure 1.1 shows a Create an Account page ready for action.

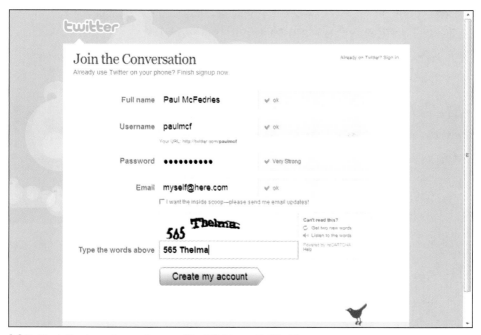

I.I Twitter's Create an Account page with all fields neatly filled in

7. **Click Create my account.** Twitter does just that, and it then offers to look for your friends on services such as AOL and Hotmail.

8. **You learn how to do this in Chapter 4, so click Skip this step.** Twitter displays a list of famous, semi-famous, or just plain infamous people who are on Twitter and asks if you want to follow them.

9. **Again, you learn how to follow the famous in Chapter 4, so click Skip this step.** Do *not* click Finish here, or else you'll end up following all 20 people! Twitter finalizes your account and drops you off on your Twitter home page.

Signing In to Your Twitter Account

With your shiny, new Twitter account fully formed and primed for action, you're ready to venture into the Twitterverse. Twitter is kind enough to deliver you to your home page right after it creates your account, so if that's where you are now you can skip ahead.

However, after you end your browser session and start a new one, you'll need to sign in to your Twitter account once again. Follow these steps to not only sign in, but also to tell Twitter to remember your credentials so you don't have to bother with this again (at least when using the same browser on the same computer):

1. **Send your trusty Web browser to https://twitter.com/login.** You can also click the Login link that appears on just about every Twitter page.

2. **Type your Twitter username in the Username text box.**

3. **Type your Twitter password in the Password text box.**

4. **Select the Remember me check box.** This tells Twitter to add a cookie to your computer that saves your username and password, which enables you to log in automatically in the future.

5. **Click Sign in.**

6. **If you started off in some other Twitter page, Twitter redisplays that page, so click Home to get to your account's home page.**

Viewing Twitter's Current Status

Twitter puts the fun in funky and the hip in friendship, but it can also sometimes put the ugh in ugly. I'm talking here about Twitter's occasional reliability problems. Twitter's original infrastructure wasn't built to handle the massive amounts of traffic it now bears, so every so often there will be a hiccup, a glitch, or even an outright failure.

These failures arise when Twitter's server simply gets overloaded, so it can't process any new data until some processing power is freed up. You know this is the case when you try to do something on Twitter and you see, instead, the infamous *fail whale*, shown in figure 1.2.

1.2 If Twitter gets overwhelmed by updates, the impossible-not-to-love fail whale shows up to let you know.

The good news is that the fail whale's moment on the stage is almost always mercifully brief, so you should be able to continue what you were doing in a few seconds or, at most, a few minutes. You'll also be happy to know that our friend the fail whale shows up far less often than he (she?) used to. Over the past few months, Twitter has made impressive strides in not only plugging the leaks but also shoring up the foundations, so the service is now more reliable than ever.

Unfortunately, that doesn't mean it's 100% reliable (online, nothing is). The fail whale still drops by unannounced on occasion, but Twitter also suffers from other gremlins from time to time. For example, you might see the whimsically mysterious "Something is technically wrong" page, shown in figure 1.3, if Twitter blows the online equivalent of a gasket.

So it pays to keep on top of Twitter's current status. There are a couple of ways you can do this.

First, send your Web browser to http://status.twitter.com/ to open the Twitter Status page, which displays updates on Twitter woes and worries, as shown in figure 1.4.

1.3 If a wrench gets thrown into the Twitter works, you might see this page.

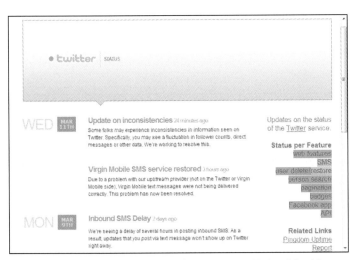

1.4 Drop by the Twitter Status page to keep an eye on Twitter's health.

Alternatively, visit the @twitter account by checking out http://twitter.com/twitter, shown in figure 1.5.

Ideally, you should follow @twitter so you see the service updates automatically. See Chapter 4 to learn how to follow folks on Twitter.

1.5 Check out the @twitter account for the latest updates on the Twitter service.

If you are wondering about the @ symbol that appears periodically through the book, know it's a kind of Twitter shorthand that means "the Twitterer with the username." So @twitter means "the Twitterer with the username twitter."

Changing Your Twitter Password

When you forged your new Twitter account, you had to specify an account password, and Twitter is security-minded enough to rate your password on-the-fly: Weak, Good, Strong, or Very Strong. If you settled for a Weak or even just a Good rating, you might be having second thoughts and feel you'd sleep better at night with a Strong or even a Very Strong password.

Conversely, you might be wondering what's the big whoop about a Twitter password? After all, it's just your Twitter account. It's not like you're exposing your finances or national security secrets to the world (I'm assuming here you're not the Secretary of State). True enough, but it's also true that Twitter accounts have been hacked in the past, with the accounts of Britney Spears and a Twitter staffer (who was using the password "happiness," which is about as weak as they come) being the most notorious. If you're using your real name with your Twitter account, then you definitely don't want some malicious hacker having his way with this part of your online identity.

Fortunately, changing the password for your Twitter account isn't much harder than what you had to go through in the first place:

1. **Sign in to your Twitter account.**

2. **Click Settings.** The Settings page appears.

3. **Click the Password tab.**

4. **Use the Current Password text box to type your existing Twitter password.**

5. **Type your new password in the New Password and Verify New Password text boxes.**

6. **Click Change.** Twitter updates your account with the new password.

Resetting Your Twitter Password

Okay, so you've been on vacation for a couple of weeks, or your nose has been grindstone-bound while you finish off a few projects, and so you've been away from the Twitterverse for a bit. It happens even to the most dedicated Twitterers. You return to the login screen and, doh!, you've forgotten your password. You try all your old favorites, but no joy. You're locked out of your Twitter account!

Fortunately, all is not lost. You can ask the kind folks at Twitter to reset your password, which will get you back up and tweeting in just a few minutes. Here's what you do:

1. **Send your Web browser to https://twitter.com/account/resend_password.** The Forgot your password? page appears.

2. **Type your Twitter username in the text box.** You can also type the e-mail address that you associated with your Twitter account.

3. **Click Reset my password.** Twitter ships you an e-mail message (Subject line: "Reset your Twitter password") that includes a link to a password reset page.

4. **When you get the message, click the link.** Your default Web browser pops up and takes you to the password reset page.

5. **Type your new password in the New Password and Verify New Password text boxes.**

6. **Click Change.** Twitter resets your account with the new password.

Deleting Your Twitter Account

I have the feeling that you're going to love Twitter, but it's also true that microblogging isn't for everyone. The constant pressure to answer the canonical Twitter question "What are you doing?" may simply become too much after a while. If taking a short break doesn't help (I'm talking about a few days or even a few weeks, not a few minutes), then you can walk away and move on with your life. You could opt to let your account lie dormant (it is, after all, free), but if there are updates you want to get rid of, or if you don't want new people to follow you, then you should delete your Twitter account.

Of course, it could be that you love the whole Twitter thing, perhaps even to the extent that you've created multiple Twitter accounts. Lots of people juggle multiple Twitter identities (I have two, myself), but it requires lots of logging in and out, and lots of extra work updating and maintaining each account. If it all just gets to be too much, you might want to delete one or more of your accounts so you can finally get some sleep at night.

If you need to go the multiple-account route, then I strongly suggest using a third-party tool that supports multiple Twitter accounts, such as twhirl. See Chapter 8 for a look at some of these powerful tweeting tools.

Fortunately, unlike a lot of online services that bury their account removal features in some obscure nook or cranny of their site (or, worse, require you to call the company to have your account terminated), Twitter makes it nearly painless to delete an account. Here's what you do:

1. **Sign in to your Twitter account.**

2. **Click Settings.** The Settings page appears.

3. **Click the Account tab.**

4. **Near the bottom of the page, click the Delete my account link.** The Delete page appears, which asks if you really want to go through with this.

5. **Click Okay, Fine, Delete My Account.** Twitter deletes your account.

Did you click the Okay, Fine, Delete My Account button and then immediately regret your rash decision? Not to worry, because Twitter actually keeps your account in limbo for six months. If you change your mind within that time, you can get your deleted account restored with almost no fuss.

1. **Direct your nearest Web browser to http://twitter.com/account/deleted**.

2. **Use the text box to type the username or e-mail address associated with the account**.

3. **Click Restore my account.** You'll receive an e-mail message that offers a link, and you click that link to restore your account.

Yes, it is really that easy, providing you restore it when your account is still in that limbo period.

What Can I Do to Customize My Twitter Profile?

1 2 3 4 5 6 7 8 9

When you first sign up with Twitter, your account is about as barebones as it gets. You have no updates, no replies, no direct messages, no followers, and no one that you're following. Zeroes across the board! You soon fix all that. For now, though, you need to get ready to meet your public. This means taking a few minutes to customize your Twitter profile by filling in some of the missing details, choosing your all-important picture, sprucing up your Twitter home with colors and a background image, and configuring how Twitter notifies you of account events.

Filling In Your Profile Details

When you created your Twitter account, you only had to specify three things about yourself: your name, the Twitter username you preferred, and a password for your account. That made the signup procedure blessedly quick, but it doesn't give folks much to chew on when they access your profile. Fortunately, Twitter lets you fill in a few more details after your account is set up, including your time zone, your Web site address, a short bio, your location in the real world, and the language you prefer. Of these, your Web address, bio, and location are the most important because they appear directly on your Twitter home page (as does your real name), so anyone (even non-Twitterers) can see them.

Here are the steps to follow to fill in these profile details:

1. **Sign in to your Twitter account.**

2. **Click Settings.** The Settings page appears.

3. **Click the Account tab.**

4. **If you want to adjust your real name, edit the Name text box.** Remember that other Twitter users usually rely on the real name to find people, so don't be shy about using your full name (although remember that you only get 20 characters to play with here).

5. **If you want to change the e-mail address that Twitter uses to communicate with you, edit the Email text box.** Although you may be tempted to use a fake address here, stick with a legit address to ensure not only that you get notifications from Twitter, but also so you have the option of resetting your password if you forget it (as I described in Chapter 1).

6. **Use the Time Zone list to choose the option that most closely matches your time zone.**

7. **If you have a separate Web site or blog, use the More Info URL text box to type the address.**

8. **In the One Line Bio text box, type a short description of yourself.** Somewhat oddly, Twitter gives you 160 characters here; limiting this field to 140 characters would seem more in keeping with the Twitter vibe, but there you go.

Give a bit of time and thought to your Twitter bio. When people are deciding whether to follow you, they look at your recent updates, for sure, but most folks also glance at the bio to get a sense of who you are. If your bio is uninspiring, people might think your tweets will be, too. A bio that portrays a sense of whimsy or fun is always welcome in the Twittersphere.

9. **Use the Location text box to type your city, state, country, GPS coordinates, or any combination of the four (up to 30 characters).** Figure 2.1 shows an Account tab with the various fields filled in.

10. **Click Save.** Twitter updates your profile.

2.1 Click Settings, and then use the Account tab to fill in your Twitter profile.

To take a peek at your newly renovated profile, click the Profile link. (If you don't see the Profile link, click Home, first, and then click Profile.) Figure 2.2 shows a Twitter profile page with the account's real name, location, Web site address (as a link), and bio.

2.2 Your profile page proudly displays your name, location, Web site address, and bio.

Setting Your Twitter Picture

If the eyes are the windows of the soul, your Twitter picture is the window of your account. Sort of. To see what I mean, check out the list of Twitterers shown in figure 2.3 (this is a list of the people a particular account is following). See the picture in the lower right corner? That's the generic image that Twitter displays when a user hasn't taken the time to choose his or her own picture.

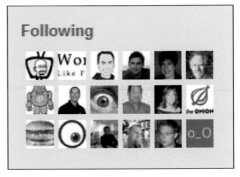

2.3 The image in the lower right corner is what Twitter displays when an account has no picture set up.

Of course, no one's going to put a gun to your head to force you to put up your own picture, but that generic image is rather lame, and it tells folks that you haven't got your act together enough to spend the couple of minutes that it takes to set your own picture. Even better, choosing your own picture is a chance to have a bit of fun. Most Twitterers use simple head shots of themselves, but a large percentage use something else entirely: a cartoon character, a caricature, an animal, a logo, or whatever. Feel free to let your imagination run a bit wild here.

Once you've settled on an image that suits your style, follow these steps to add it to your profile:

1. **Sign in to your Twitter account.**
2. **Click Settings.** The Settings page appears.
3. **Click the Picture tab.**
4. **Click Browse.** If you're using Safari, click Choose File, instead. A file selection dialog box appears.
5. **Choose the file you want to use, and then click Open (or Choose in Safari).** You can use either a JPEG or a PNG file, and the maximum size is 700KB.
6. **Click Save.** Twitter updates your profile with the new image.

Although you might think you need to use a tiny image for Twitter, you can load a larger image if you want. Twitter shrinks it down to size in your profile, but folks can click the image to see it full-size.

Applying a Theme to Your Profile

Your fresh-out-of-the-box Twitter account sets up your pages to use a collection of colors and images that are the same for all new accounts:

- The page background is light blue.
- The page background shows faint cloud-like images.
- The sidebar uses a light green background.
- The sidebar border is a slightly darker green.
- The links are a darker blue.
- The text is dark gray.

Taken together, these half dozen items comprise the profile's theme. Happily, you're not stuck with the default theme. If you want to give your Twitter profile a different look, you can apply one of the dozen prefab themes that Twitter provides, or you can take an even more customized approach by choosing your own theme components.

The next couple of sections take you on this theme road less traveled, but for now here are the steps to follow to apply a predefined Twitter theme:

1. **Sign in to your Twitter account.**
2. **Click Settings.** The Settings page appears.
3. **Click the Design tab.**
4. **In the Select a theme area, click a theme that looks promising.** Twitter applies the theme temporarily, as shown in figure 2.4.
5. **Repeat step 4 until you find a theme that suits you.**
6. **Click Save Changes.** Twitter updates your profile with the new theme.

2.4 Click a theme thumbnail and Twitter applies the background and colors temporarily.

Selecting a Background Image

Applying a predefined Twitter theme is an easy way to escape the standard-issue look of a freshly minted Twitter account, but it doesn't exactly scream "rugged individualist." If you really want to stand out from the Twitter herd, then you need to customize your theme with your own background and (as I describe later), your own color scheme.

You may be wondering at this point why you should bother taking the time and trouble to build a custom theme. First, as you'll soon see it doesn't take all that much time and almost no trouble. Second, even if it doesn't bother you to stick with a cookie cutter theme from Twitter, it's not going to impress other Twitterers, and that may be the deciding factor when they're choosing whether or not to follow your tweets (which are the updates you post). After all (a Twitterer might say), if you can't be bothered to do something original and interesting with your theme, then perhaps your updates won't be all that original and interesting, either. Myself, I think that most Twitterers decide on who to follow based on the quality of a person's updates, not on the appeal (or lack thereof) of their theme, but certainly there's no harm in making your Twitter home look nice.

Using a solid color background

The simplest customization you can make to your design is to switch to a solid color background. Swirling patterns and striking photos have their place in the world of Twitter backgrounds, but some people find them distracting. Framing your Twitter home with an attractive color lays a solid foundation for your content, and focuses your reader's attention on your posts.

 Because the update background is always white, you can give your profile an attractively clean and classily simple look by switching to a white background.

Here are the steps you have to follow to switch to a solid color background:

1. **Sign in to your Twitter account.**

2. **Click Settings.** The Settings page appears.

3. **Click the Design tab.**

4. **If you have a predefined Twitter theme applied, click Change background image, and then click Don't use a background image.**

5. **Click Change design colors.**

6. **Click the Background swatch.** Twitter displays two color controls, as shown in figure 2.5. The outer circle controls the base color, and the inner square controls the amount of gray in the color.

7. **Click a spot in the outer circle to set the base color.** You can also drag the small circle to set the base. When you make your choice, Twitter temporarily changes the background color so you can see the results.

 If you happen to know the color code of the shade you want, you can type it directly in the Background swatch. Be sure to use the format #*rrggbb*, where *rr* is a two-digit hexadecimal value (00 to 99 and AA to EE) that specifies the red component, *gg* is a two-digit hexadecimal value that specifies the green component, and *bb* is a two-digit hexadecimal value that specifies the blue component.

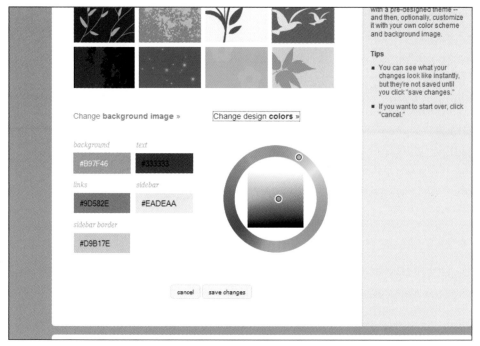

2.5 Click Change design colors and then use the color pickers to choose the color you want.

8. **Click a spot in the inner square to set the gray component color.** You can also drag the small circle to set the grayness. Again, Twitter temporarily changes the background color so you can see the results.

9. **Click Save Changes.** Twitter updates your profile with the new background color.

Selecting a custom background image

If you want to ramp up the "wow" factor, if you want to use your Twitter profile as part of a personal or business branding strategy, or if you just want a Twitter home that truly reflects your style and personality, then you need to augment your design with a custom background image.

You might think this is just a simple matter of uploading your favorite photo, but Twitter offers several unique challenges when it comes to selecting a background image. Before I get to those, run through the steps you need to follow to apply a custom background image to your Twitter profile:

1. **Sign in to your Twitter account.**

2. **Click Settings.** The Settings page appears.

3. **Click the Design tab.**

4. **Click Change background image.**

5. **Click Browse.** If you're using Safari, click Choose File, instead. A file selection dialog box appears.

6. **Choose the file you want to use, and then click Open (or Choose in Safari).** You can use either a JPEG or a PNG file, and the maximum size is 800KB.

7. **If you want Twitter to tile the image to cover the background, select the Tile background check box.**

8. **Click Save Changes.** Twitter updates your profile with the new background image.

After you save your profile, you might end up on the "Something is technically wrong" page or even the fail whale page. This is an annoyingly common problem, and the best solution is to keep refreshing your browser until Twitter gets its act together. Note that when you refresh, your browser asks whether you want to resubmit the form, so be sure to choose yes.

Background photo challenges

As I mentioned earlier, Twitter presents a couple of hurdles that you need to leap over when selecting a background image. First, the Twitter content area — the box in the middle of the screen that displays your updates and the Twitter sidebar — is a "fixed" target that you have to work around. I put "fixed" in quotation marks because it does move from side to side as you change your browser width or screen resolution, and it does expand vertically as you add updates to your profile and as you start receiving other people's tweets. However, the content area is fixed in three other ways:

- It's always centered on the screen.
- It's always the same width: about 760 pixels.
- It's always located in the same position vertically: about 70 pixels from the top of the page.

This means that your background image has got to deal with a distressingly large object. For example, on a screen with a resolution of 1024 × 768 with the browser window maximized, as shown in figure 2.6, you have about 120 pixels of open area to the left of the content box and about 120 open pixels to the right of the content. You also have about 70 pixels open above the content box, but that area is partially blocked by the Twitter logo and the site navigation tools.

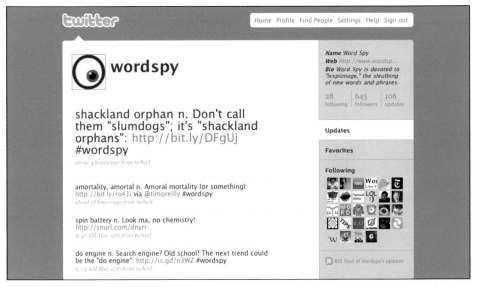

2.6 On a typical screen, you only get a bit of room around your content to show off a background image.

So if you want to use a photo as your background, then even if you use an image large enough to cover the screen, the bulk of the image will be blocked, which is going to be a problem for most photos. For example, check out the Twitter page shown in figure 2.7. You see part of a floating dock on the right, and a splash on the left, but the key part of the image (it's a dog in midair after diving off the dock) is blocked by the content area.

If you want to use a photo as your Twitter background, a better idea is to use a scene where the action isn't just in the middle of the image. A beach shot, landscape, or similar image where the subject either extends across the photo or offers visual interest on the edges is a good way to go. Figure 2.8 shows an example.

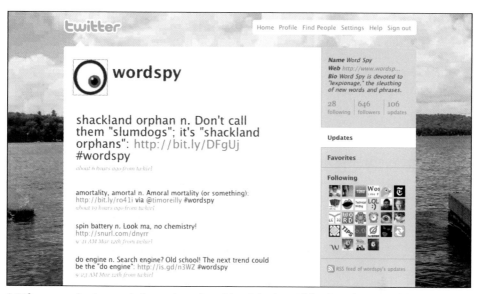

2.7 If you use a background photo where the subject is in the middle, the subject gets blocked by the Twitter content box.

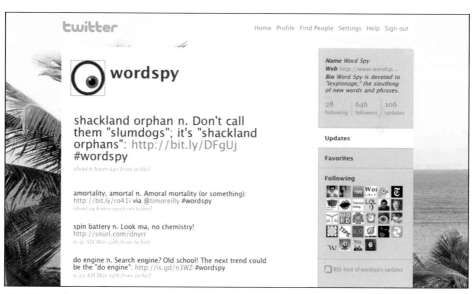

2.8 A Twitter background where the existence of the content box doesn't spoil the effect

The second challenge you face when choosing a background is the size of the image you select. If you use a relatively small image, Twitter displays it in the upper left corner of the screen, and then fills in the rest of the background with your chosen background color. That's not terrible if your background color goes well with your image, but it's not optimum, either. Twitter does offer an option to tile the background, but few photos look good when tiled.

To work around this problem, you should use a relatively large background image, and by relatively large I mean a photo with dimensions that are larger than the browser window. This means the background color never appears, and you don't have to worry about tiling the image. Of course, this leads to yet another problem: how large? According to the firm Market Search, as of December 2008 the percentage of users running their screens at various display resolutions broke down as shown in Table 2.1.

Table 2.1 Display Resolution Percentages

Resolution	Percentage of Users
1024 × 768	36.66
1280 × 800	19.68
1280 × 1024	12.68
1440 × 900	8.30
1680 × 1050	5.48
800 × 600	4.49
Other	12.77

As you can see, the most popular resolution is 1024 × 768, but more than 32 percent of users run their screens at 1280 pixels wide. So if you assume a maximum width of 1280 pixels, then you've got about 80 percent of the market covered (assuming some of those in the "Other" category are running at 640 × 480). This means that you should resize your photo to a width of at least 1280 pixels. What if you don't want anyone to see the background color? Then you need to use a width of 2048 pixels, which is about the widest screen that anyone runs nowadays.

What about height? Again, you want to make sure that your photo's height is greater than the display height of most of your users. From Table 2.1, you can see that if your photo's height is at least 1050 pixels, then you'll cover almost everyone. Again, if you want to be sure that no one sees your background color, go with a height of 1556 pixels.

You may be wondering how a 1050-pixel-high image will work when your profile extends down the page with your updates and your friends' tweets. The secret here is that Twitter displays your background image with fixed positioning, so the content area scrolls as you scroll the browser window, but the background remains in place. So as long as the photo is taller than the browser window, no background color appears at the bottom of the screen.

Using a background image to tell people more about yourself

The one-line bio that Twitter includes as part of your profile is limited to a relatively pathetic 160 characters. My life certainly can't be summarized in such a teensy space, and I'm sure yours can't, either. To work around this limitation, many Twitterers offer more information about themselves using their profile backgrounds. How? By taking advantage of the gap that most users see to the left of the content box. With a little graphics program know-how, you can create your own background image that includes a picture and some text in a vertical strip that runs down the left side of the image. Make this strip background the same color as your Twitter background, and you've got yourself a nice background *and* a chance to tell people more about yourself.

How wide should you make this strip? Because most folks use a display resolution of at least 1024 × 768, then almost everyone who visits your Twitter page will see at least a 120-pixel gap to the right of the content box (assuming they're running their browser window maximized). So make your strip 120 pixels wide, add a nice picture that's the same width, and use your graphics program's text tool to add some text that runs down the strip. Figure 2.9 shows an example (which includes an added design bonus: a 70-pixel-high strip across the top), and figure 2.10 shows the background applied to a Twitter profile.

 The specifics of creating the background image vary depending on the graphics program you use and the tools it offers. One basic procedure is to create a new image that's the height and width you want, and then fill that image with the background color you want. Then use the shape-drawing tool to create a rectangle that's 120 pixels wide and the same height as the background. You can then use the text tool to overlay your text on the rectangle.

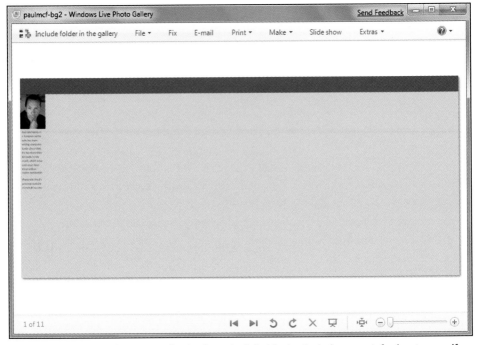

2.9 Create an image with a 120-pixel strip along the left side that includes more info about yourself.

2.10 The image from figure 2.9 applied as a Twitter background

It's a good idea to test your custom background on a variety of browsers at a variety of display resolutions. If that sounds like way too much work, head over to Browser Shots (http://browsershots.org/) and choose the browsers and screen sizes you want to test.

Overcoming background problems with tiling images

If you really don't want to get into the hassle of worrying about photo sizes, display resolutions, and creating a custom background from scratch, you can get a blissfully problem-free background by applying an image with a pattern that tiles gracefully. Even better, there are plenty of sites out there that either offer ready-made patterns that you can download, or that enable you to generate your own patterns.

For simple pattern downloads, check out the following sites:

- TweetStyle: http://tweetstyle.com
- Twitter Backgrounds Gallery: http://twitterbackgroundsgallery.com
- Twitter Background Images: www.twitterbackgroundimages.com
- Twitter Gallery: http://twittergallery.com
- Twitter Patterns: www.twitterpatterns.com

If you prefer to come up with your own pattern, here are a few pattern generators you can try out:

- BgPatterns: http://bgpatterns.com
- Colour Lovers: www.colourlovers.com
- Dotted Background Generator: www.pixelknete.de/dotter/
- Stripe Generator: www.stripegenerator.com
- Stripe Mania: www.stripemania.com
- Tartan Maker: www.tartanmaker.com

Choosing Your Profile's Colors

The last bit of design customization you need to perform is to select the colors you want to use for four other aspects of your profile: the text, the links, the sidebar background, and the sidebar border. Here's how it's done:

1. **Sign in to your Twitter account.**

2. **Click Settings.** The Settings page appears.

3. **Click the Design tab.**

4. **Click Change design colors.**

5. **Click the Text swatch.** Twitter displays two color controls, as shown in figure 2.11. The outer circle controls the base color, and the inner square controls the amount of gray in the color.

2.11 Click Change design colors, click a color swatch, and then use the color controls to choose the color you want.

6. **Click a spot in the outer circle to set the base color.** You can also drag the small circle to set the base. When you make your choice, Twitter temporarily changes the background color so you can see the results.

7. **Click a spot in the inner square to set the gray component color.** You can also drag the small circle to set the grayness. Again, Twitter temporarily changes the background color so you can see the results.

You can also type a color code directly into the swatch. Use the format #*rrggbb*.

8. **Repeat steps 5 to 7 for the Links, Sidebar, and Sidebar border swatches.**

9. **Click Save Changes.** Twitter updates your profile with the new colors.

Stopping Twitter from Sending New Follower Messages

With all these great renovations you've been doing, it won't be long before people start beating a path to your Twitter door. You'll know right away if your custom design is a hit because Twitter sends you an e-mail message every time a kind soul decides to follow you. Personally, I love getting these messages because it's great to know that my tweets have a growing audience, and it also gives me a chance to check out lots of other profiles. You never know who you might come across and decide to follow yourself.

On the other hand, if your profile becomes quite popular, getting tons of messages from Twitter may not appeal to you. Similarly, you might be following as many people as you can handle, so you're not interested in also following any of your new followers.

If that's the case, then you should follow these steps to tell Twitter to stop sending you an e-mail message each time someone follows you:

1. **Sign in to your Twitter account.**

2. **Click Settings.** The Settings page appears.

3. **Click the Notices tab.**

4. **Deselect the Email when someone starts following me check box.**

5. **Click Save.** Twitter updates your profile with the new setting.

How Do I Send Twitter Updates?

1 2 3 4 5 6 7 8 9

Twitter begins with nearly the simplest question you can imagine: What are you doing? From that deceptively humble beginning, the entire edifice that is the Twittersphere emerges, because it's through these updates — or *tweets* as most Twitterers prefer to call them — that you open up part of your life for other people to see; stay connected with family, friends, and far-flung co-workers; share interesting things you've found online; and learn new things from those intrepid Twitterers that you follow. This chapter introduces you to the surprisingly deep world of the Twitter update.

Sending an Update

There are a few folks with Twitter accounts who are "read-only" users: they follow others, but they don't post any updates themselves. That's fine, I guess, if you've simply got nothing to say, but few of us are that tongue-tied. I assume you signed up with Twitter because you've got some things to share, so the next few sections take you through a few ways that you can do just that.

Before you get to that, you may be wondering exactly what you should be posting. Are there any rules, official or unofficial, for the type of content that you can send? Fortunately, the answer to that question is a resounding "No!" If what you have to say isn't illegal, then go ahead and say it. Of course, you only have 140 characters to work with, so Twitter is no place for the long-winded. The sheer compactness of a typical Twitter missive means that although the content is as varied as the people who send it, tweets do tend to fall into a few basic categories:

- **Simple status updates.** These are the purest of the tweets because they're the ones that answer the "What are you doing?" query literally. When Twitter began in 2006, this kind of update comprised the vast majority of tweets, but that has been changing recently, and the tweet types that follow are becoming more prominent as Twitter morphs under the sheer weight of its users.

In a March 2009 interview with the online magazine SuicideGirls (http://suicidegirls. com/), Twitter CEO Evan Williams said that he "wouldn't be surprised" if Twitter someday changed the "What are you doing?" question to something that more accurately reflects how people use Twitter today. His favorite alternative question is "What's happening?".

- **Link to an interesting site.** This is a tweet that provides a short description of some interesting, fun, or useful site, followed by the site's address. These types of updates are becoming increasingly common, and they're a great way to learn new things and to find out about obscure Net nooks that you might otherwise have missed.

- **Link to your own content.** This type of tweet lets your followers know when you've published something elsewhere on the Web. If people like your tweets, then chances are they may also like your blog posts, Flickr albums, or other online content that you create.

- **Conversations.** These tweets are back-and-forth exchanges between two or more people. This is when Twitter becomes very much like an instant messaging system.

- **Broadcasts.** These are tweets with a specific type of content sent on a regular schedule. "Word of the day" (see for example @thewordoftheday and @awordaday) and "Quotation of the day" (such as @quotesoftheday and @quotesnak) tweets are good examples.

- **News.** These can be personal "Here's something good (or bad or interesting or whatever) that has happened to me recently" updates, to the latest news stories sent by professional media organizations.

- **Live-tweeting.** This refers to sending on-the-fly updates that describe or summarize some ongoing event. The most common live-tweeting scenario is an announcement, speech, or panel discussion at a conference or media event, but live-tweeting is becoming increasingly common at major events, such as the Oscars and U.S. President Barack Obama's inauguration, and breaking news stories, such as the 2008 terrorist attacks in Mumbai, India.

Sending an update using the Twitter site

There are multiple ways you can post updates to Twitter, and you learn about most of them elsewhere in the book. However, the most common posting method is still the Twitter site itself, so run through the steps:

1. **Sign in to your Twitter account.**

2. **Click Home.**

3. **Use the large What are you doing? text box to type your update.** As you type, the number above the right edge of the text box counts down from 140 to tell you how many characters you have left. There are three things to note about this countdown:

   - When the count dips below 20, the number color changes to Maroon.

   - When the count dips below 10, the number color changes to Red.

   - When the count dips below 0, the number color stays Red, but it also sprouts a negative sign, and Twitter disables the Update button, as shown in figure 3.1. You need to get the count back to 0 or more before Twitter allows you to post.

4. **Click Update.** Twitter posts the update and adds it to the feed of every person who's following you.

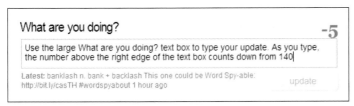

What are you doing?   **-5**

Use the large What are you doing? text box to type your update. As you type, the number above the right edge of the text box counts down from 140|

Latest: banklash n. bank + backlash This one could be Word Spy-able:
http://bit.ly/casTH #wordspyabout 1 hour ago   update

3.1 If you exceed your 140-character allotment, Twitter lets you know by showing a negative number of characters remaining.

Interesting or useful updates often get *retweeted* — passed along to another person's followers. This is a good thing because it gets your Twitter identity passed around, so consider making your posts retweet-friendly. A retweet consists of the abbreviation RT, followed by @*username* (where *username* is the username of the original tweeter), and then the update text. To ensure all this fits inside the retweet, consider making your tweets a maximum of 120 characters. This is explained in more detail in Chapter 4.

Tips for managing the 140-character limit

If there's one thing that even many non-tweeters know about Twitter it's that its messages can be no more than 140 characters long. Why 140 and not, say, 200, or 500, or no limit at all? Twitter was designed originally to use the Short Message Service (SMS) to send out its updates, and on the majority of SMS systems at the time, each message was limited to 160 characters. Twitter's messages had to tack on the username at the front (which can be up to 15 characters long), so it chose 140 characters as the limit for a Twitter update.

Of course, knowing why you've only got 140 characters to express your thoughts is one thing, but actually shoehorning that thought into such a tiny space is quite another. Fortunately, with a bit of practice you'll find yourself getting remarkably adept at crafting 140-words-or-less gems. To help you get there, here are a few pointers to bear in mind when composing your updates:

- **Take advantage of the symbol short forms that are built in to the language**. Use & or + instead of "and," $ instead of "dollars," % instead of "percent" or "percentage," and so on.

- **Use common abbreviations.** E-mail, chat, instant messaging, and other forms of Internet communication have created a wide variety of abbreviations and acronyms, many of which are in common use: BTW (by the way), FYI (for your information), LOL (laughing out loud), and TTYL (talk to you later). Don't hesitate to use these and other familiar short forms to save characters.

- **Find shorter words.** If there's a key to winning the battle with the 140-character limit, it's this: if a word has a shorter synonym, use the synonym. Delete "perturbed" and replace it with "mad"; get rid of "therefore" and use "so," instead; replace "supercalifragilisticexpialidocious" with "cool."

- **Avoid redundancy and wordiness.** If you're bumping up against the 140-character ceiling, cast a critical eye over your text and ruthlessly rewrite passages that are redundant or that use more words than necessary. For example, use the Delete key to change "in the vicinity of" to "near" and trash "at this point in time" in favor of "now."

● **Be precise.** Twitter is no place to waste words. Your tweets should encapsulate a single thought, idea, action, reaction, or event, and they should discuss that one thing in a way that gets right to the point and says only what needs to be said.

● **Shorten your URLs.** It's not unusual these days for Web addresses to be long-winded affairs that consume dozens of precious characters. To knock a URL down to size, use a URL shortening service such as TinyURL (http://tinyurl.com/), Snurl (http://snurl.com/), or bit.ly (http://bit.ly/). See Chapter 9 to learn more about URL shortening.

Typing non-standard characters in Twitter

Besides the keys that you can eyeball on your keyboard, you can also include in your tweets a few non-standard characters, such as € and ™. Twitter supports a character set called UTF-8, which is a list of 400 symbols, from the usual alphanumeric suspects to currency symbols, math operators, foreign characters, and more. Table 3.1 presents a few useful characters and their corresponding codes.

Table 3.1: Characters You Can Use In Your Twitter Posts

Character	Code	Character	Code
€	Alt+0128	®	Alt+0174
…	Alt+0133	±	Alt+0177
•	Alt+0149	^{2}	Alt+0178
™	Alt+0153	^{3}	Alt+0179
¡	Alt+0161	$^1/_4$	Alt+0188
¢	Alt+0162	$^1/_2$	Alt+0189
£	Alt+0163	$^3/_4$	Alt+0190
¥	Alt+0165	×	Alt+0215
©	Alt+0169	÷	Alt+0247

To type one of these characters, hold down Alt and type the four-digit code using your keyboard's numeric keypad.

Alternatively, use the Character Map application in Windows:

1. **Choose Start ⇨ All Programs ⇨ Accessories ⇨ System Tools ⇨ Character Map.** The Character Map window appears.

2. **Double-click the symbol you want to use.** Character Map adds the symbol to the Characters to copy text box.

3. **Click Copy.** Character Map copies the character to the Clipboard.

4. **Switch to your Web browser and position the cursor within the Twitter text box at the position you want the character to appear.**

5. **Press Ctrl+V.** Windows pastes the character into the text box.

You can also enter special characters online. Check out a neat tool called TwitterKeys (http://thenextweb.com/2008/09/16/twitterkeys-enhance-your-twitter-conversations/) which offers a pop-up window with nearly 200 useful symbols that you can copy and paste into Twitter's update text box.

Notes on tweet etiquette

Twitter is a freeform service that doesn't have a whack of rules to follow, and that lack of regulation is a big part of Twitter's appeal for many people. However, that doesn't mean that anything goes on Twitter. Like other forms of online communication, Twitter has evolved a loosely defined set of guidelines that together form a kind of Twitter etiquette (which, inevitably, some folks refer to as *Twittiquette*). There's no definitive list of these do's and don'ts, but some common etiquette ideas have emerged over the past few years. For posting tweets, here are a few etiquette guidelines to consider:

- **Don't send spam.** Nobody wants to see a sales pitch in their timeline, so avoid updates that market products or services.

- **Don't overtweet about your other content.** It's perfectly acceptable to let your followers know when you've put content up on some other site, such as your blog. However, if that's all you do, then people will stop following you. Make sure you use Twitter to post original material.

- **Do give credit.** If another person's tweet leads you to find something interesting and you then share that interesting tidbit with your followers, be sure to give a tip of the hat to the original poster. This doesn't have to be anything elaborate. Somewhere in your tweet, just add "via @*username*" or "thanks @*username*," where *username* is the account name of the original tweeter.

- **Don't post private information.** Never include phone numbers, addresses, or other private data (yours or someone else's) in a tweet. Remember that all your updates appear, albeit briefly, on Twitter's public timeline, which means that anyone, anywhere in the world can see what you post.

- **Don't overshare.** Some folks get so excited about Twitter that they seem to post every thought that pops into their head. Not only are even your closest friends and family members unlikely to read so many tweets but, even worse, a large number of updates in a short period of time pushes other people's updates off each of your follower's personal timelines, and that's just rude.

- **Do treat your fellow tweeters with respect.** Twitter has a fun and relaxed vibe that mostly stems from the respect that most Tweeters show each other, and so rude exchanges between users are rare. Do your part to keep Twitter beautiful by keeping your tweets civil and respectful.

Adding hashtags to create a tweet topic

A stream of incoming tweets is typically a real mishmash of people, personalities, and topics, and that's part of the fun and excitement of Twitter. However, every now and then you get a series of tweets centered around a particular topic. It might be an ongoing event, a TV show or movie, or a broader cultural idea such as New Year's resolutions. If you're seeing lots of tweets on a particular subject from your friends, then it's likely that all kinds of other Tweeters are talking about the same topic. That means there's likely to be tons of great information about the subject floating around the Twittersphere. That's great, but how do you get your mitts on that info?

You could use the Twitter search engine to track down the relevant tweets, but Twitter offers a much easier method: hashtags. A *hashtag* is a keyword (preceded by the hash symbol — # — hence the name) associated with a particular subject, and Tweeters include the hashtag in any tweet on that subject.

For example, as I write this the SXSW (South by Southwest) festival is happening, and the hashtag for that event is #sxsw. So if someone posts a tweet about SXSW, they include the hashtag #sxsw somewhere in the update. This serves to tag the tweet as SXSW-related, so anyone looking for SXSW tweets needs only to use the Twitter search engine to look for that hashtag.

If you want to use hashtags in your own posts, note that you first need to follow @hashtags by going to http://twitter.com/hashtags and clicking Follow. This user follows you back automatically, and it then indexes your hashtags.

To track the most popular hashtags, go to http://hashtags.org/, shown in figure 3.2.

3.2 You can see the most popular hashtags by visiting the hashtags.org site.

Working with Your Updates

Once you've begun posting updates in earnest, you may find that you need to perform a little maintenance work from time to time. Twitter doesn't offer many options in this department, but there are three things you can do: delete an update, mark an update as a favorite, and make your updates private. The next three sections take you through the details.

Deleting an update

One of the unusual and occasionally frustrating quirks of Twitter is that your tweets aren't editable. Once you click the Update button, your post gets shipped out to all your friends and what they see is what you sent. If you misspelled a word, made some egregious grammatical gaffe, or forgot to include an address or some other crucial bit of data, too bad; the flawed tweet remains in the Twittersphere for all to see.

When they make a major mistake in an update, most Tweeters simply send a fresh copy of the tweet with the corrections made (and, if possible, a brief note about what was corrected). Still, that error-filled tweet remains in the timeline. What to do? The one thing that Twitter does allow you to do is delete a tweet. This removes the tweet not only from your profile page (which lists all your tweets), but also from the timelines of everyone who follows you.

Here are the steps to follow to delete an update:

1. **Sign in to your Twitter account.**

2. **Click Profile.** Twitter displays a list of your recent tweets.

3. **If you don't see the tweet you want to remove, scroll down to the bottom of the page and click Older.** Repeat this until you find the update.

4. **Move the mouse pointer over the tweet text.** As you can see in figure 3.3, the Delete this update icon (a garbage can) appears to the right of the tweet.

3.3 Hover the mouse over a tweet's text to see the Delete this update icon.

5. **Click the Delete this update icon.** Twitter asks you to confirm the deletion.

6. **Click OK.** Twitter removes the tweet from your profile page, as well as from the home pages of all of your followers.

A deleted tweet is gone for good, and no amount of crying, caterwauling, or calls to Twitter tech support will get it back. Double-, no, triple-check that you want to blow away the tweet before confirming the deletion.

Adding an update to your favorites

Twitter saves copies of all your updates on your profile page. The most recent 20 tweets appear on the main profile page (log in to your account and click Profile). To see earlier tweets, click the Older link at the bottom of the page, and then you keep clicking Older to go farther back in your update history.

This is fine if you only check out your previous tweets from time to time. However, you might occasionally post an update that contains something really useful that you want to access frequently, such as a Web site or a quotation. In that case, it can be a real pain to always have to dig back through your tweets to find the update you're looking for. To work around this problem, Twitter lets you save that tweet as a favorite, and you can access it quickly by clicking the Favorites link that appears on both your home page and your profile page.

Here are the steps required to save one of your tweets as a favorite:

1. **Sign in to your Twitter account.**

2. **Click Profile.** Twitter displays a list of your recent tweets.

3. **If you don't see the tweet you want to save as a favorite, scroll down to the bottom of the page and click Older.** Repeat this until you find the update.

4. **Move the mouse pointer over the tweet text.** As you can see in figure 3.4, the Favorite this update icon (a star) appears to the right of the tweet.

5. **Click the Favorite this update icon.** Twitter adds a copy of the tweet to your Favorites list.

Twitter also changes the Favorite this update icon to an orange Un-favorite this update icon. As you've no doubt guessed, you click this icon when you no longer want to store a tweet in your Favorites list.

Making your updates private

A default Twitter account is pretty much an open book:

- Anyone (even people without a Twitter account) can access your home page and view your tweets.

- Each time you post a tweet it appears briefly on Twitter's public timeline for all the world to see.

- Anyone with a Twitter account can follow your updates.

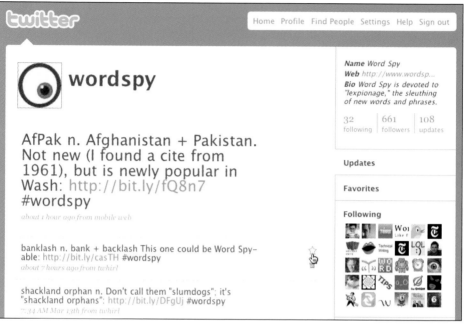

3.4 Hover the mouse over a tweet's text to see the Favorite this update icon.

Most Tweeters are fine with this, but you might prefer a less open approach. If so, you can configure your Twitter account to protect your updates. This means your account is much more private:

- Only people who follow you can access your home page and view your tweets.
- Your tweets never appear on Twitter's public timeline.
- People who want to follow you must send a request, and you can then either approve or decline that request.

If you like the sound of all that, here are the steps to follow to protect your updates:

1. **Sign in to your Twitter account.**
2. **Click Settings.** The Settings page appears.
3. **Click the Account tab.**
4. **Select the Protect my updates check box.**
5. **Click Save.** Twitter updates your profile to protect your updates.

Now when a non-follower tries to access your Twitter home page, he or she sees the message shown in figure 3.5.

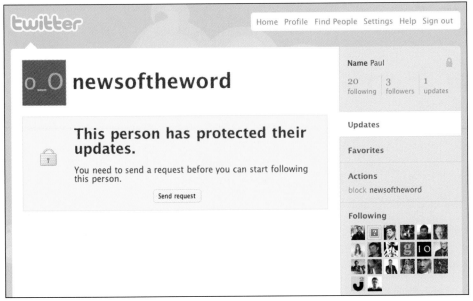

3.5 With your Twitter account protected, non-followers see this message instead of your tweets.

 Twitter also sends you an e-mail message letting you know you have a follower request. That message includes a link that you can click to accept or decline the request. If you want to turn this e-mail option off, see Chapter 2.

If that person wants to follow you, he or she must click the Send request button. When that happens, you see a "1 new follower request!" message in the Following section of your home page, as shown in figure 3.6. Click that link and then click either Accept or Decline.

Downloading All Your Updates

Your Twitter updates appear in your profile pages, so you always have access to all your tweets. However, once you've posted a few dozen updates or more, it's a hassle to slog

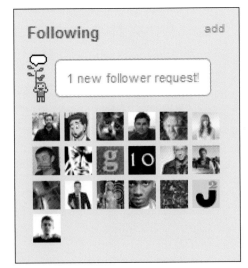

3.6 When your Twitter account is protected, you can approve or deny follower requests.

through a bunch of different pages in your profile to find the post you want. You can use the Twitter search engine (see Chapter 6) to track down the post, but that's a bit of a hassle.

The other problem with having the posts stored in your profile pages is that although this serves as a rough-and-ready backup, do you *really* trust Twitter to keep your tweets safe?

If you want easier access to your tweets, and you want to preserve a local backup copy of your updates, then you need to download your updates to your computer. You can do this right from your Web browser by entering a special address that uses the following general syntax:

http://twitter.com/statuses/user_timeline/*account.xml*?count=*n*

Here, replace *account* with your Twitter username, and replace *n* with the number of tweets you want to return. If you want to return all your updates, log in to your account, check your total number of updates (it's available on both your home page and your profile page), and then plug that number into the above address as the count value.

 As I write this, the maximum value for the count parameter appears to be the oddly specific value of 982. If you use a value larger than that, you get an error message.

What you get in return is a page chock full of data in the XML (extensible markup language) format, as shown in figure 3.7.

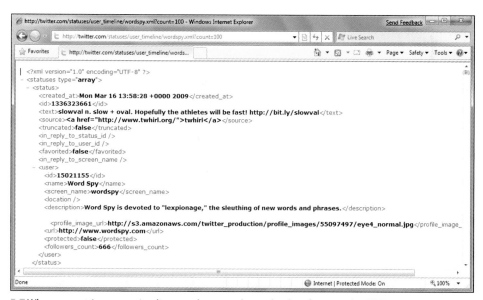

3.7 When you retrieve your timeline, you browser shows the data formatted as XML.

Now you save the data by choosing File ⇨ Save As, choosing a location and file name in the Save As dialog box, and then clicking Save.

 If you'd prefer to receive your tweets in the slightly more friendly comma-separated values (CSV) file format, check out Tweet Scan (www.tweetscan.com), which offers a download feature. It requires you to enter your Twitter username and password, but it's safe because it doesn't store your data.

If you have Excel 2007, you can import the XML file into a worksheet for easier viewing, searching, and so on. Here's how:

1. **In Excel, click the Data tab.**

2. **In the Get External Data group, choose From Other Data Sources ⇨ From XML Data Import.** The Select Data Source dialog box appears.

3. **Navigate to the XML file location, click the file, and then click Open.** Excel tells you it will create a scheme for the file.

4. **Click OK.** Excel prompts you for a location to import the data.

5. **Click the cell where you want the data to appear, and then click OK.** Excel displays the XML data in a table.

6. **Choose File ⇨ Save As, and then use the Save As dialog box to save the data as an Excel workbook.** Consider using the Save as type list to choose the Excel 97-2003 file format for maximum compatibility. Figure 3.8 shows just such a file loaded into the Mac version of Excel.

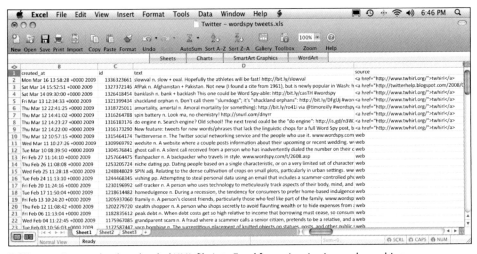

3.8 You can import the downloaded XML file into Excel for easier viewing and searching.

Downloading your tweets is easy, but this method suffers from a glaring problem: as soon as you start posting tweets again, your backup becomes out of date, so you need to perform regular downloads. However, it doesn't make sense to download all your tweets each time. You could adjust the count value based on the number of updates you've sent since the last download, but Twitter offers an easier way. If you examine figure 3.7 (and figure 3.8), you see that each tweet is given a unique ID value. You can use the value to download just those tweets you've posted since your last download. You do that by using your Web browser to enter a special address that uses the following general syntax:

http://twitter.com/statuses/user_timeline/*account*.xml?since_id=*ID*

Again, *account* is your Twitter username, and *ID* is the ID value for the latest tweet in the previous download. For example, in figures 3.7 and 3.8, you can see that the latest tweet in my @wordspy account has the ID value of 1336323661, so I could download every tweet since that post by using the following address:

http://twitter.com/statuses/user_timeline/wordspy.xml?since_id=1336323661

Working with Replies and Direct Messages Sent to You

Although at first it looks like Twitter is a one-way medium — you fire off your tweets and that's the end of it — it probably won't take long before you realize that's decidedly not the case. Twitterers are a garrulous bunch, and they don't hesitate to chime in with their couple of cents' worth. They do that either by replying to one of your tweets, or by sending you a direct message. The next few sections show you how to handle the replies and direct messages that come your way.

Viewing replies sent to you

If another tweeter comes across one of your updates and that person has a response, a retort, or a rebuttal (or simply wants to congratulate you on your wisdom and insight!), he crafts a reply. (You learn how to do this yourself in Chapter 4.) That reply appears on his personal timeline, but your timeline remains resolutely unaffected (unless you're following him). So how do you see the replies sent to you? By following these steps:

1. **Sign in to your Twitter account.**
2. **Click Home.**
3. **In the sidebar, click @Replies.** Twitter displays a list of all the replies that have come your way, as shown in figure 3.9.

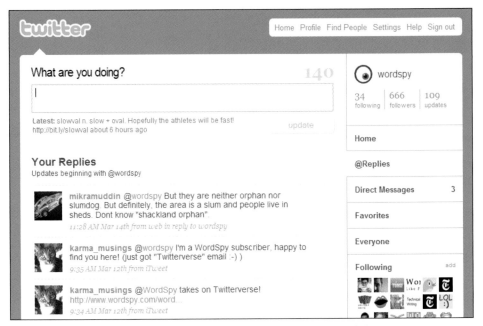

3.9 On your home page, click @Replies in the sidebar to see the replies people have sent you.

Viewing direct messages sent to you

If you're in a *mutual follow* Twitter relationship — that is, a person follows you and you also follow that person — then that person can send you a *direct message*, which is a private note that only you see. (Many tweeters refer to direct messages as directs.) That is, the direct message doesn't appear on your timelines, so you must follow these steps to read it:

1. **Sign in to your Twitter account.**

2. **Click Home.**

3. **In the sidebar, click Direct Messages.**

4. **Click the Inbox tab.** Twitter displays a list of all the direct messages you've received, as shown in figure 3.10.

twitter

Home   Profile   Find People   Settings   Help   Sign out

Send [⌄] a direct message.   140

Send

Inbox   Sent

Direct Messages Sent Only to You

MrTweet Hi there! Mr Tweet, your personal Twitter assistant is ready for work. Meet him here: http://mrtweet.net/home/wor...
4:48 AM Mar 13th

twanslate Thanks for following @twanslate! Send me direct messages to get translations, see http://twanslate.com for details!
9:50 AM Mar 11th

Wo1   Wordie Thanks for following Wordie! Visit http://wordie.org for the latest words.
Like F   *8:44 PM Mar 10th*

wordspy

34   666   110
following followers updates

Home

@Replies

Direct Messages   3

Favorites

Everyone

Following   add

3.10 In your home page sidebar, click Direct Messages to see the directs people have sent you.

Getting an e-mail when you receive a direct message

If someone you're following replies to one of your updates, then you see that reply in your friend timeline, but for all other replies you must open the @Replies section of your home page. However, direct messages never appear in your timelines, so you must sign in to Twitter to see them. That's a hassle, but luckily it's possible to configure your Twitter account to forward direct messages to your e-mail address. This option is turned on by default in new Twitter accounts, but it's worth following these steps to make sure:

1. **Sign in to your Twitter account.**

2. **Click Settings.**

3. **Click the Notices tab.**

4. **Select the Email when I receive a new direct message check box.**

5. **Click Save.** Twitter updates your account with the new setting.

How Do I follow Other Twitter Users?

1 2 3 **4** 5 6 7 8 9

Twitter would be just another lonely outpost on the fringes of the Web if all anyone ever did was post tweets. Twitter is, instead, a vibrant, noisy place because it goes beyond mere microblogging and embraces its social side by letting you follow other tweeters. This means that you subscribe to that person's updates, which then appear on your home page, so you can easily keep track of what that person shares with the Twitterverse. By following your pals, family, colleagues, and even total strangers that you find inexplicably fascinating, and by replying to tweets, exchanging messages with your friends, and sending friends' tweets to your followers, you begin to get the full measure of the Twitter experience.

Finding People

As you see a bit later, to follow someone on Twitter, you must usually access that person's Twitter page. That's fine and all, but how do you find someone's page? If you don't know anyone on Twitter (or, probably more accurately, if you haven't yet discovered people you know on Twitter), how do you find someone to follow? Fortunately, Twitter offers a number of features that make it fairly easy to find people you know or people who are worth following. The next few sections provide the details.

Finding people with Twitter accounts

The best way to get started is to use the Find on Twitter feature, which enables you to scour the database of tweeters for someone you know. You can search by first name, last name, or even the person's Twitter username. Here's how it works:

1. **Sign in to your Twitter account.**
2. **Click Find People.** The Find People page appears.
3. **Click the Find on Twitter tab.**
4. **Use the text box to type the name (first or last or both) of the person you're looking for.** Using both first and last names is usually the way to go here. If that doesn't work, use just the last name or the first name, whichever is more unique. If all you have is a partial username, you can enter that instead.
5. **In the search results, click the person's avatar or username to check out their profile.**

Finding someone on another network

Searching for the members of your posse individually using the Find on Twitter feature is an easy way to get going, but it can be time-consuming and frustrating if you keep coming up empty. An often better way to go is to get Twitter to do some of the legwork for you. Specifically, you can tell Twitter to rummage through your list of contacts on your Gmail, Yahoo!, AOL, Hotmail, or MSN account. If Twitter finds one or more tweeters, it displays them in a list.

Follow these steps to give this a whirl:

1. **Sign in to your Twitter account.**
2. **Click Find People.** The Find People page appears.

3. **Click the Find on other networks tab.**

4. **Click the network you want to scour: Gmail, Yahoo, AOL, Hotmail, or MSN.**

5. **Type the e-mail address and password for that account, as shown in figure 4.1.**

If you feel a bit queasy at the thought of handing over your account credentials to Twitter, then good for you for having some security common sense. Many social networking services offer a similar feature, and you should never dole out third-party login data willy-nilly. Check the site's privacy policy, and only provide your credentials if you trust the site.

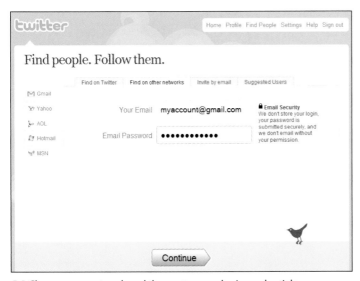

4.1 Choose your network and then enter your login credentials.

6. **Click Continue.** Twitter connects to your account, downloads your contacts list, and then checks for matches in the Twitter database. If it finds any, it displays them in a list and selects the check box beside each person by default.

7. **If there are any people you don't want to follow, deselect the check box beside each of those people.**

8. **Click Follow.** Twitter displays the Why not invite some friends? page, which lists all your contacts who don't have a Twitter account. You can use this list to extend invitations to one or more contacts to join Twitter.

9. **Select the check box beside each person you want to invite.**

10. **Click Invite.** Twitter fires off an e-mail message to each person.

Inviting someone to join Twitter

Many people enjoy Twitter so much that they want to share the experience with their close friends, respected co-workers, and the saner members of their family. Other tweeters have a hard time finding anyone they know on Twitter, so it becomes a bit of a lonely place. Whichever camp you find yourself in, you can share Twitter with people you know by sending them an e-mail invitation to join the service. The message that Twitter sends on your behalf looks like this:

```
From: Your Name Here
Subject: Your Name Here wants to keep up with you on Twitter
To find out more about Twitter, visit the link below:
http://twitter.com/i/0f6fc06f0d52c55f25246b7316ea81c5324564a6

Thanks,
-The Twitter Team

About Twitter

Twitter is a unique approach to communication and networking based on the
simple concept of status. What are you doing? What are your friends
doing right now? With Twitter, you may answer this question over SMS or
the Web and the responses are shared between contacts.
```

When your friends click the link, they see your Twitter profile page with a link to join up.

If this sounds like a plan, follow these steps to send out the invitations:

1. **Sign in to your Twitter account.**

2. **Click Find People.** The Find People page appears.

3. **Click the Invite by email tab.**

4. **Use the large text box to type the e-mail address of the person you want to invite.** If you want to fire off multiple invites, separate each address with a comma, as shown in figure 4.2.

5. **Click Invite.** Twitter dispatches an e-mail message to each address.

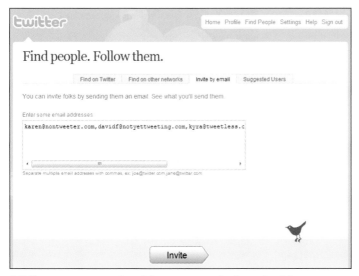

4.2 Choose your network and then enter your login credentials.

Tracking FollowFriday recommendations

Following people you know is a big part of Twitter's appeal, and it adds an irresistible personal touch to the service. However, although I'm sure your friends and family are fascinating, it's a vast Twitterverse, and it's teeming with smart, funny, engaging people whose tweets just might improve your day if you followed them. But how on earth do you find these people? The best way is by asking the tweeters you do know for suggestions. Just post an update asking your followers who they recommend, and then check out the resulting tweeters as the responses come in. (In any Twitter post, if you see @ followed by a username, you can click that username to view the person's profile.)

A more indirect way to canvass your followers is to check out who they follow. On your home or profile page, click the Followers link, click a username, and then click the person's Following link. I've found perhaps a third of the people I follow using this method.

That should get you a few good recommendations, but why stop at just your followers when you can get the entire Twitosphere involved? Well, perhaps not everyone, but at least every tweeter who knows about FollowFridays. This is a Twitter topic where every Friday people post one or more updates that recommend a particularly good tweeter. Each update includes the #followfriday hashtag, so all FollowFridays are easily found and searched. Here are a couple of ways you can track FollowFriday updates:

- **Use Twitter search.** You can use Twitter's advanced search feature to search for a particular hashtag. I talk about this in detail in Chapter 6, but for now you can plug the following address into your Web browser: http://search.twitter.com/search?q=%23followfriday.

- **Use TopFollowFriday.** This site tracks the most endorsed tweeters, either on the current day or all-time: http://topfollowfriday.com/.

Following People

The best way to revel in another person's Twitter goodness is to follow that person. Sure, you can simply use your Web browser to dial up a person's Twitter profile and read their stuff, but you lose the immediacy of seeing their updates arrive in your timeline, and you miss out on some of the social aspects of Twitter (such as not being able to send a message directly to that person).

Following someone on Twitter

Following someone on Twitter usually takes just a single click, but what you click depends on where you are in the Twitter interface. There are two possibilities:

- **Viewing a person's profile page.** In this case, look for the Follow button under the person's avatar. Twitter replaces the Follow button with a Following notice, as shown in figure 4.3.

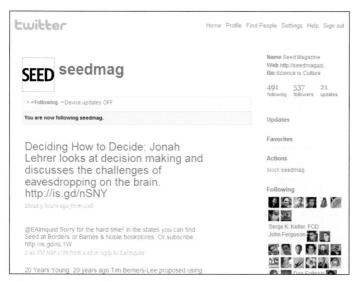

4.3 In a tweeter's profile page, click the Follow link and Twitter changes your status to Following.

Viewing a list of followers or friends. In this case, each tweeter in the list has a Follow button, and you click that button to follow that person. Twitter removes the Follow button and displays You are now following *username* (where *username* is the person's Twitter screen name), as shown in figure 4.4.

note If instead of a Follow button you see the message This person has protected their updates, it means the user must approve your follow request. Click the Send request button to make the request.

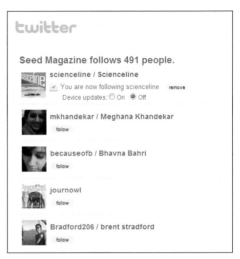

twitter

Seed Magazine follows 491 people.

scienceline / Scienceline
✓ You are now following scienceline   remove
Device updates: ○ On ● Off

mkhandekar / Meghana Khandekar
follow

becauseofb / Bhavna Bahri
follow

journowl
follow

Bradford206 / brent stradford
follow

4.4 In a list of followers or friends, click a tweeter's Follow link and Twitter changes your status, as shown here.

Following Twitter's suggested users

If you're really not sure where to start with this following business, then you might want to take a look at Twitter's Suggested Users page, which lists over 100 Twitter users. The list is a real mixed bag that includes mostly members of the Twitterati (the Twitter elite who have the most followers) — including celebrities, companies, media outlets and personalities, and bands — plus the odd apparently randomly selected tweeter. It's not exactly personal, but it's an easy way to populate your friend timeline.

note To keep track of the most popular tweeters, check out Twitterholic at http:// twitterholic.com.

Here are the steps to follow:

1. **Sign in to your Twitter account.**

2. **Click Find People.** The Find People page appears.

3. **Click the Suggested Users tab.** Twitter displays a list of users.

4. **Select the check box beside each person you want to follow.** Twitter adds the user's avatar under the You'll be following heading, as shown in figure 4.5.

5. **Click Follow.** Twitter returns you to your home page and you see the latest messages from your selected users in your friend timeline.

If you want to dive into the deep end, select the Select All check box to select every suggested user.

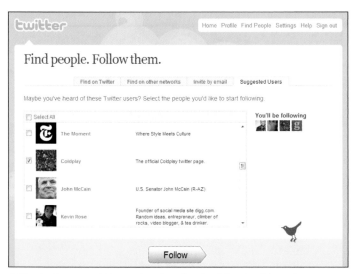

4.5 In the Suggested Users tab, select the check box beside each user you want to follow.

following a person's updates via RSS

If you're a dedicated blog follower and find yourself spending more time in your RSS reader than just about anywhere else, you might not like the idea of having to access the Twitter site or even sign in to your Twitter account to follow a particular person's tweets. Similarly, you might be following someone's tweets and you don't want to miss a thing while you're not signed in to Twitter. In both cases, Twitter makes each user's timeline available in an RSS feed, so you can add that feed to your favorite RSS reader. Twitter even makes it easy to subscribe to the feed using Live Bookmarks, Bloglines, Google, or My Yahoo!. Here's how it works:

1. **Sign in to your Twitter account.** Actually, this part is optional because you don't need to be logged in to access someone's RSS feed. However, if you want to get the feed for one of your friends or followers, then you need to sign in.

2. **Navigate to the user's profile page.**

3. **In the sidebar, click the RSS feed of *username*'s updates link, where *username* is the user's screen name.** Twitter displays the feed, as shown in figure 4.6.

4. **Subscribe to the feed.** The steps required here vary depending on your RSS reader. The standard technique is to copy the feed URL in the browser's address bar, navigate to your RSS service, select the option to add a feed, and then paste the feed address.

 If you want to follow all your friends via RSS, sign in, and then click Home to display your friend timeline. In the sidebar, click the RSS feed link and then enter your Twitter login credentials in the dialog box that appears

4.6 A Twitter user's RSS feed

Following people who follow you

One of the ongoing debates in Twitter circles involves the question of whether you should always follow someone who follows you. Many tweeters believe that it's rude not to follow someone who has been kind enough to sign up for your tweets. After all, that person has indicated they're interested in what you have to say, so by not reciprocating you're effectively saying you're not interested in what they have to say. Not only that, but Twitter's direct message feature (which I discuss in just a bit) requires that two users follow each other. Believe it or not, many Twitter geeks examine a user's *follow ratio*, which compares the number of people that user follows with the number of people that follow the user. A low follow ratio means that a person follows few people compared to how many follow her, and to many tweeters, that's a bad sign.

Other tweeters counter that Twitter isn't (or shouldn't be) a numbers game. Your friend timeline should be a reflection of your interests, your work life, or your social life (or even all three), and automatically adding tweeters to your list of friends defeats that purpose because you're bound to get deluged with updates you're completely uninterested in, or even offended by. Even worse, if you're lucky enough to become popular on Twitter, do you really want your timeline to be inundated with the tweets from hundreds or even thousands of users, the vast majority of whom you don't know from Adam?

Which side of the fence you come down on in this debate really depends on what you want to get out of Twitter. If you want to keep in touch with friends, family, and a few tweeters that you've found interesting or entertaining, then follow who you want; if you want the complete social experience that Twitter provides, follow everyone who comes your way.

Following someone who is following you

If you decide to go the latter route, then Twitter offers a couple of methods you can use to follow a person who is now following you:

- **E-mail link.** Assuming you've configured Twitter to send you an e-mail message each time someone follows you, display that message in your e-mail program, and then click the link to view the person's profile. When the profile loads in your Web browser, click the Follow button.

- **Twitter site.** Load your home page or profile page, click your followers link, and then click the Follow button beside the user.

Automatically following someone who follows you

Following your followers manually isn't a big deal if you only receive a few friend requests per day. However, if your Twitter profile takes off, you might become insanely popular and start receiving dozens of new followers each day. That's a nice position to be in, for sure, but you could end up spending vast chunks of your day just processing all those new fans.

To avoid that, you can use a powerful online tool called TweetLater to automatically follow anyone who follows you. Go to www.tweetlater.com and sign up for a free registration. (There's a paid version of the service, but you don't need it for this.) Once you've done that, you add your Twitter account and then configure it to automatically follow your followers. Because TweetLater is an online service, the interface changes fairly regularly. However, here are the steps to follow as I write this:

1. **Log on to your TweetLater account.**
2. **Click the +Twitter tab.** The Add a New Twitter Acocunt page appears.

3. **Type your screen name in the Twitter User Name text box.**

4. **Type your password in the Twitter Password text box.**

5. **Select the Auto Follow check box, as shown in figure 4.7.**

6. **Click Save.** TweetLater adds your accounts and configures it to automatically follow your followers.

Optional Twitter Account Automation

Auto Welcome:	☐ Automatically send a welcome message to new followers.
Message Sending Method:	All welcome messages are sent as Direct Messages.
Send This Message:	
	Maximum 120 characters.
	Best Practise: The message should not be about you, it should be about your follower and your future interaction with your follower.
	Write a very simple welcome message. If you really want folks to unfollow you, then try and sell them something with this first welcome message. Very few people like that. Be careful even if you're giving away something for free. The purpose of this message is to say hello and welcome. Most people take a dim view of you when you do any kind of self-promotion with this message. If your message smells remotely like, "Hi, thanks for the follow, now buy my stuff or do something that will benefit me or check out how cool I am," then you really are misusing this welcome message. Don't send what you wouldn't like to receive from others.
Auto Follow:	☑ Automatically follow people (new followers) who follow me from this point forward.
Vet Followers:	☐

4.7 Add your Twitter account to TweetLater and select the Auto Follow check box.

As I write this TweetLater waits about 12 hours before processing your new followers, and it then checks your account a couple of times a day to look for new followers. TweetLater does not process your existing followers, so if you want to follow them you must do it manually.

Downloading your friends' tweets

If you're a bit behind on your friends' updates and you're looking for a way to catch up while you're offline, this usually requires a Twitter client such as the programs I discuss in Chapter 8. However, if you're willing to wrestle with some XML code, then here's another method you can use:

1. **In your Web browser, type the following address, where you replace *n* with the number of updates you want to retrieve:**

http://twitter.com/statuses/friends_timeline.xml?count=*n*

2. **Press Enter or Return.** The Twitter server prompts you to log on to your account.

3. **Enter your Twitter username and password.** The browser displays the updates in XML format. See Chapter 3 to learn how to import an XML file into Excel 2007.

 There are also many XML viewers available for free. Google "XML viewer" and you'll get lots of hits.

Stopping following someone on Twitter

Unfortunately, it's a fact of Twitter life that not everyone is interesting! Some people take the What are you doing? question too much to heart, some people are rude, and some people simply over share. Whatever the reason, if someone's updates are clogging your timeline, it's best to "defriend" that person by stopping following them. There are two ways you can do this:

4.8 Tweeter displays this message when you remove a user.

- **Viewing your list of followers.** Sign in to your account, click either Home or Profile, and then click Followers. Locate the person you want to get rid of, and then click the Remove button. Twitter tells you you're no longer following that user, as shown in figure 4.8.

- **Viewing a person's profile page.** In this case, click Following to display the extra controls shown in figure 4.9, and then click Remove.

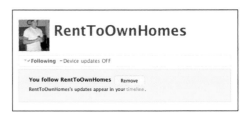

4.9 On the user's profile page, click Following and then click Remove.

 Twitter doesn't tell you when people quit following you. If you want to know, sign up with Qwitter at http://useqwitter.com/.

Replying, Retweeting, and Direct Messaging

Twitter is a social network, and part of what that entails is the exchange of messages between tweeters. This is mostly achieved by posting updates that then appear on the friend timelines of the folks who follow you, but Twitter also offers three other ways to create conversations and exchanges: replying to an update; retweeting an update; and sending someone a direct message. The next three sections tackle the specifics.

Replying to an update

A *reply* is a response to a tweeter's update, and that response appears on your timeline, as well as on the original tweeter's timeline. You usually send replies to people you follow, but on Twitter anyone can send a reply to anyone (as long as that person's account isn't protected). Send a reply when you have a comment about a tweet, you want to follow up on a tweet, or you have new information about a tweet.

Here are the steps to follow to reply to an update:

1. **Sign in to your Twitter account.**

2. **Locate the update you want to reply to.** The update might appear on your friend timeline, in your mentions timeline, a tweeter's timeline, the Twitter public timeline, or in the result of a Twitter search.

3. **If the update appears in a timeline, hover the mouse pointer over the update.** Twitter displays the Reply to *username* arrow (see figure 4.10, where *username* is the name of the person who posted the tweet). If the update appears in a list of Twitter search results, you see a Reply link instead.

4.10 Hover the mouse pointer over a tweet to see the Reply icon.

4. **Click the Reply icon.** If you're working with search results, click the Reply link instead. Twitter displays the Reply to *username* text box and adds @*username* to the box (where, in both cases, *username* is the tweeter's screen name).

5. **Type your reply as shown in figure 4.11.** Feel free to add text either before or after the *@username* text. Twitter will recognize the tweet as a reply as long as you have the *@username* text somewhere within the update

6. **Click Reply.** Twitter posts the reply, which then appears in your update timeline as well as in the user's mentions timeline.

Reply to BelkinB: **18**

@BelkinB "Sufficience" sounds new, but the OED has citations going back
as far as 1380! Thanks for the suggestion, though.|

Latest: RT @chr1sa: More new...jargon: "calenderize". [T]o   reply
schedule things that should happen at a ... about 2 hours ago

4.11 Type your response in the Reply to *username* text box.

If you can't find the tweet you want to reply to, don't sweat it because you can still send a reply as long as you know the tweeter's username. Sign in to your account, and then click Home. In the What are you doing? text box, type *@username*, where *username* is the tweeter's screen name. When you press space, Twitter changes the text box name to Reply to *username*. Now type your response and click Reply.

Retweeting an update

A *retweet* is another person's tweet that you copy and send out to your followers, along with an acknowledgment of the original tweeter. You most often retweet updates from the people you follow, but you're free to retweet anyone's updates. Retweet an update if you think it will be especially interesting or relevant to the people who follow you.

The curious thing about retweeting is that, unlike replying and direct messaging, it's *not* an official Twitter feature! It's just something some intrepid tweeters starting doing a while back, and now it's a standard part of the tweeter's posting arsenal. (When you learn about various Twitter clients in Chapters 5 and 8, you see that most of them now come with "Retweet" features.)

A retweet is an update that uses the following general form:

```
RT @username: original tweet [your comment]
```

Here, *username* is the name of the original tweeter; *original tweet* is the text of the update you're retweeting; and *your comment* is text that you add to comment on the update. Note, first of all, that this format isn't the only way to retweet. Some folks add their comments to the beginning, some people put the username at the end, while others use "retweet" or "retweeting" instead of RT.

Here's the basic procedure for retweeting an update:

1. **Sign in to your Twitter account.**

2. **Locate the update you want to retweet.** The update might appear on your friend timeline, in your mentions timeline, a tweeter's timeline, the Twitter public timeline, or in the result of a Twitter search.

3. **Copy the tweet text, including the username at the beginning of the tweet.**

4. **Click Home.**

5. **Click inside the What are you doing? text box.**

6. **Type RT.** If you want to post only part of the original tweet, use PRT (partial retweet) instead.

7. **Type a space and then @.**

8. **Paste the text you copied in step 3.**

9. **Type your own text (if you have room) after the original tweet text.** Figure 4.12 shows a retweet ready to ship.

10. **Click Update.** Twitter posts the retweet, which then appears in your update timeline.

4.12 A typical retweet

To keep track of the most popular retweets and the most retweeted users, check out Retweetist at http://retweetist.com.

In a few cases you might want to retweet a reply that someone has sent you. For example, if a tweeter asks you a question, you might want everyone who follows you to see the answer. In that case, most people use the following format to retweet a reply:

```
From @username: original reply [your comment]
```

You want to exercise some caution and a bit of common sense when retweeting replies. Although replies are public in the sense that they appear on the responder's timeline, don't retweet any reply that contains personal information or that you think the responder wouldn't want shared with a broader audience. When in doubt, ask permission with a direct message (if you also follow that person) or a reply.

What if you come across a tweet that contains an interesting idea or a useful link, but you don't want to quote the original tweeter verbatim? For example, you might have your own spin on the original topic and so you want to post your thoughts along with the link. In that case, it's proper Twitter etiquette to acknowledge the original tweeter by including somewhere in your update the text "via @*username*", where *username* is the screen name of the original tweeter.

Sending a direct message to someone

A *direct message* is a note that you send directly to a tweeter, where "direct" means that the message doesn't appear on either your timeline or the recipient's timeline. You can only send a direct message to someone if the two of you follow each other. Send a direct message when you want a private exchange with someone.

How you send a direct message depends on where you are in the Twitter landscape:

- If you're viewing the list of people you follow, you see a Direct message link beside each person that also follows you. Click the Direct message link for the person you want to contact.

- If you're on the profile page of a mutual follower, click the Message link in the Actions section of the sidebar.

- If you're viewing your Direct Messages timeline (click Home and then click Direct Messages in the sidebar), use the Send *x* a direct message list to choose your recipient (see figure 4.13).

Whichever message you use, Twitter displays a text box. Type your message in the box, as shown in figure 4.13, and then click Send.

4.13 After you choose your recipient, type the message and click Send.

If you're having a hard time finding the person you want to direct message, you don't need to use the Twitter interface to find them. If you know the person's username, you can click Home and use the What are you doing? text box to type a message that uses the following general format:

d *username message*

Here, *username* is the screen name of the person you want to write to, and *message* is your text. When your message is ready, click Send to ship it.

Finally, if someone sends you a direct message, you might feel like writing back. The easiest way to do this is through your Direct Messages timeline (click Home, and then click Direct Messages in the sidebar). Hover the mouse over the message you want to respond to; then click the envelope icon shown in figure 4.14. Type your response in the text box and then click Send.

4.14 Hover the mouse pointer over a direct message to see the envelope (reply) icon.

To keep your Direct Messages timeline less cluttered, delete any messages you no longer need. Hover the mouse pointer over the message, and then click the trash can icon. When Twitter asks you to confirm the deletion, click OK.

Configuring direct message e-mails

When you follow someone and that person also follows you, then the two of you can send direct messages to each other. Because direct messages are more personal, Twitter automatically configures your account to send any direct messages you receive to your e-mail address. If you want to turn off this feature, or if you like the idea and want to make sure this setting is activated, follow these steps:

1. **Sign in to your Twitter account.**

2. **Click Settings.** Your Twitter account settings appear.

3. **Click the Notices tab.**

4. **To get direct messages via e-mail, select the Direct Text Emails check box.**

5. **Click Save.** Twitter configures your account with the new setting.

Configuring your reply settings

When someone includes your @*username* text anywhere in an update, the tweet shows up in your mentions timeline (click Home, and then click @*username* in the sidebar). These mentions can be from people who follow you or non-followers who happened to stumble across your tweet.

What about the people you follow? That is, because you normally see their tweets in your friend timeline, do you also see the replies they send out to other people? The answer is that it depends on who they reply to:

- If a person you follow replies to another person you follow, then the reply shows up in your friend timeline.

- If a person you follow replies to a person you don't follow, then the reply doesn't appear in your friend timeline.

This configuration makes sense when you think about it. For example, suppose you follow Kyra and David, and Kyra replies to one of David's tweets. Because you're following both people, then chances are you saw David's tweet that Kyra is replying to, so you probably understand (or can figure out) what she's talking about in her reply. Therefore, it's reasonable for you to see Kyra's reply on your friend timeline.

On the other hand, suppose you follow Kyra but not David. In this case, you won't have seen David's original tweet, so Kyra's reply might be gibberish, so it makes sense for the reply to not appear on your friend timeline.

What I've just described is the default for Twitter's so-called @Replies setting. However, there are two other possibilities:

- **All @ replies.** This setting tells Twitter to include in your friend timeline every reply posted by the people you follow. In our example, if you follow Kyra but not David and Kyra replies to one of David's tweets, that reply appears on your friend timeline. This is a useful setting if you're interested in seeing everything posted by the people you follow.

- **No @ replies.** This setting tells Twitter to not display any replies in your friend timeline, even friend-to-friend replies. Use this setting if you only want to see original tweets.

Here are the steps to follow to configure the @Replies setting:

1. **Sign in to your Twitter account.**
2. **Click Settings.** Your account settings appear.
3. **Click the Notices tab.**
4. **Use the @Replies list to choose the setting you want, as shown in figure 4.15.**
5. **Click Save.** Twitter applies the new setting to your profile.

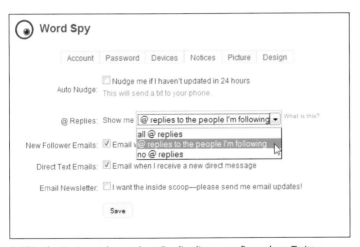

4.15 In the Notices tab, use the @Replies list to configure how Twitter handles replies.

Working with the People You follow

Once you start following people on Twitter, your interactions with them will mostly consist of reading their tweets, replying when you've got something to say, and sending direct messages to people who also follow you. However, Twitter does offer a few other choices, such as displaying a person's updates and nudging and blocking a user. The next few sections provide the details.

Checking out a person's updates

If you follow a bunch of people, a particular update from a particular user can fall off the first page of your friend timeline in a hurry. Rather than leaping through your timeline pages to locate the tweet, it's often easier to display the person's updates. This is also useful if you've been offline (or just off-Twitter) for a while and you want to catch up with a favorite friend.

Twitter gives you several ways to access a user's tweet timeline, depending on where you are in the interface:

- If you see an update from that person in your friend timeline, click the username at the start of the tweet.

- If you've got the person onscreen in your list of followers, click the username.

- Use your Web browser to type **http://twitter.com/*username***, where *username* is the Twitter screen name of the person you want to read.

Nudging a tweeter

If someone you follow hasn't updated in a while, you might find that you miss their voice and wish they'd return to tweeting. If that person also follows you, you could fire off a direct message asking what's up, but Twitter offers an easier (although less personal) method: the nudge. A *nudge* is a text message sent to your phone to remind you to post an update. The text of the message looks like this:

```
You've been nudged! Biff wants to know what you're doing. Reply to this message
   to update your Twitter friends.
```

You can only nudge someone if all of the following conditions are met:

- You both follow each other.
- The user has a mobile phone registered with Twitter.

- The user's mobile phone is on.

- The user has authorized Twitter to send text messages to his or her phone.

See Chapter 5 to learn how to register your phone with Twitter.

If you answered "check" for all four conditions, then the person is eminently nudge-able. Twitter gives you three ways to nudge someone, depending on where you are in the Twitter interface:

- If you're viewing the list of people you follow, you see a Nudge link beside each person that can be nudged. Click the Nudge link for the person you want to contact.

- On your home page, use the What are you doing? text box to type **nudge @*username***, where *username* is the Twitter screen name of the person you want to electronically elbow.

- If you're on the profile page of a mutual follower, click the Nudge link in the Actions section of the sidebar, as shown in figure 4.16.

Actions

message paulmcf
nudge paulmcf
block paulmcf

4.16 If a person is nudge-able, a Nudge link appears in their profile page's Actions section.

If you get busy, it's easy to neglect your Twitter friends while your nose is grindstone-bound. If you'd like to avoid that (but can't avoid being busy), you can get Twitter itself to nudge you to update. This is called Auto Nudge, and it is explained in Chapter 5.

Blocking a tweeter

A huge number of people use Twitter, and most of those folks seem to get the friendly Twitter vibe. Of course, anytime you're dealing with a massive crowd you're bound to come across a bad apple or three. It might be someone who's rude or offensive, a huckster using Twitter to sell snake oil, or a company that bombards you with marketing messages. In most cases, the easiest solution is to stop following the user and, if the user is also following you, to remove the person from your list of followers.

That usually works, but there's a small subset of pests who'll just start following you all over again, or who'll send you replies even if they're not following you. For these hardcore cases, Twitter offers a hardcore solution: block the user. Blocking someone means that he or she can't follow you and can't send you replies.

Twitter gives you two ways to block a user:

- If the person is currently following you, open your list of followers, and then click the Block link for the person.

- If the person isn't following you, go to his or her profile page and click the Block link in the Actions section of the sidebar, as shown in figure 4.17.

Actions

block tonyrobbins

4.17 To shut annoying tweeters out of your life, access their profile page and click the Block link in the Actions section.

Working with Twitter Bots

Twitter is home to millions of people, but it's also a place where many non-humans hang out. Yes, there are lots of companies and organizations on Twitter, but I'm talking here about a different kind of Twitter critter: the bot. A *bot* is an automated Twitter account that returns some kind of data in response to a specially formatted message. Some Twitter bots respond to reply messages, but most require direct messages, which means that you must follow the bot, and the bot then automatically follows you. (Remember that direct messaging requires mutual following. If you've protected your account, be sure to accept the bot's friend request when it comes in.)

In the rest of this chapter, I introduce you to Twitter's bot population by showing you how to interact with a few of the more useful bots.

note

Twitter bots are most useful when you've configured your account to send direct messages to you, either via e-mail (as described earlier in this chapter) or via your mobile phone (see Chapter 5).

Receiving a reminder message

Ask someone how they're doing these days, and more often than not you'll get an exasperated "Busy!" as the response. We're all up to our eyeballs in meetings, chores, and other commitments, so it's not surprising that every now and then we forget one of those tasks, and all the apologizing we have to do puts us even farther behind. Fortunately, you can use Twitter to avoid this fate. The Twitter bot named timer is an automated reminder service. You send it a direct message and a time, and when that time elapses timer sends you a direct message back.

To use timer, first go to http://twitter.com/timer and click the Follow button to follow this bot; it immediately follows you in return, so you're now set up to exchange direct messages with timer.

When you need a reminder, send a direct message to timer with the number of minutes after which you want the reminder sent (the minimum is 5 minutes), and the text you want timer to send back in the reminder message. For example, if you want to be reminded to call Karen in 30 minutes, your direct message will look like this:

```
30 Call Karen1
```

If you're using the What are you doing? text box to send the message, remember to include the d command and the timer username:

```
d timer 30 Call Karen
```

The timer bot is useful, but don't rely on it for accurate reminders. The timer bot seems to get around to sending the reminders when it's good and ready, so reminders are routinely a few minutes late.

Querying the Internet Movie Database

If you want to get some quick info on a movie or a movie personality, the famous Internet Movie Database (www.imdb.com) has a Twitter bot — named, not surprisingly, imdb — that's happy to serve. The imdb bot responds to either direct messages or reply messages.

To use direct messages, go to http://twitter.com/imdb and click the Follow button; the imdb bot follows you right back. Note, too, that the imdb account on Twitter also tweets regularly by sending out movie-related updates with themes such as Born On This Date, Trivia, and Quote.

If you don't want to receive the imdb tweets, bypass the following and send messages to @imdb instead.

If you want to get information about a movie, use the t command followed by the name of the movie:

```
d imdb t spinal tap
```

or

```
@imdg t spinal tap
```

If you know there are multiple versions of the movie, you can also specify the year:

```
d imdb t gladiator 2000
```

or

```
@imdb t gladiator 2000
```

To get information about a movie personality, use the p command followed by the person's name:

```
d imdb p clive owen
```

or

```
@imdb p clive owen
```

Getting a map

If you need a quick map of a city or town, use the Twitter 411 bot named t411. Go to http://twitter.com/t411 and click the Follow button; the t411 bot immediately follows you, too. You can now send your request using the following format:

```
d t411 map place
```

Here, *place* is the name of the city or town you want to see on a map. In response, you get a direct message with a URL. Click that address to see the map.

Translating text into another language

If you want to know how to say an English word or phrase in French, German, or some other language, or if you come across a foreign phrase that you want to convert to English, you can use the Twitter bot named twanslate. This is a direct message bot, so you first need to go to http://twitter.com/twanslate and click the Follow button. Once twanslate follows you back, you're good to go.

The first thing you should do is retrieve the twanslate help text by sending the following direct message:

```
d twanslate help
```

This text gives you the language abbreviations that you need to use in the twanslate commands. For example, the abbreviation for French is fr, so to translate the English phrase "I love Twitter" into French, you'd send the following message:

```
d twanslate fr I love Twitter
```

Getting a weather forecast

Want to know what the weather's going to be like where you are or where you're traveling to, but don't have access to a weather forecast? Now you do thanks to the Twitter bot named forecast, which can provide a forecast for a given city or a given postal code.

The forecast bot uses direct messages, so first navigate to http://twitter.com/forecast and click the Follow button. Once the forecast bot returns the following favor, you can send your message. There are two ways to use the forecast bot: by city and by postal code.

To get the weather forecast for a city, send a direct message with the following format:

```
d forecast city, state
```

Replace *city* with the name of the city, and replace *state* with the two-letter state abbreviation. For example, the following direct message returns the forecast for Indianapolis, Indiana:

```
d forecast indianapolis, in
```

To get a weather forecast for a particular ZIP or postal code, send a direct message with the following format:

```
d forecast zip
```

Here, replace *zip* with the ZIP code of the location. For example, the following direct message returns the forecast for the 46256:

```
d forecast 46256
```

Returning Amazon data

Amazon.com stores a wealth of data about millions of books, DVDs, and albums, and now all of that data is at your fingertips thanks to the Twitter bot named junglebot. This bot responds to direct messages, so first go to http://twitter.com/junglebot and click the Follow button. Once junglebot follows you back, you can use it to start querying Amazon.

You can use junglebot to return data about books, DVDs, or music using the following direct messages formats:

```
d junglebot book title
d junglebot dvd title
d junglebot music title
```

In each case, replace *title* with the name of the book, DVD, or music CD you want to work with. For example, to get information about the book *iPhone 3G Portable Genius*, you'd send the following direct message:

```
d junglebot book iphone 3g portable genius
```

Keeping up with the bots

The half dozen bots that you learn about here really only scratch the surface of a burgeoning new Twitter field. New bots seem to come online every day, so how do you keep up? Perhaps the best way is the Twittter Fan Wiki, a wiki site that monitors all-things Twitter, including bots. Check out the following page from time to time to see what's new in the Twitter bot landscape:

http://twitter.pwiki.com/Bots

Can I Use Twitter on My Mobile Phone?

1 2 3 4 5 6 7 8 9

The Twitter Web site is fine as far as sites go: it's simple to use and presents a nice, uncluttered interface. However, the fundamental element of the Twitter experience is *immediacy*: you think of or read or see something interesting, you send a tweet *now*; your friend posts an update, you read it *now*. Trying to do this on the Web isn't necessarily ideal because there are many hurdles between you and your tweets. If you want the true Twitter experience, your mobile phone is the way to go because you can post and read tweets right away, as you see in this chapter.

Understanding Twitter's Mobile Phone Feature

Twitter began life as a service for exchanging SMS (short message service) messages, so mobile phones have been at the heart of the Twitter model from day one. As long as your phone is capable of working with text messages, and as long as your mobile provider rate plan includes a text messaging component, you can send and receive tweets with your phone.

Considering text message fees

Of course, it's one thing to have a text messaging plan, but it's quite another not to go bankrupt with a text messaging plan. How you use Twitter from your mobile phone (indeed, *whether* you use Twitter from your mobile phone) depends on the text messaging rates set by your provider. There are three possibilities:

- **Your provider charges a per-message fee.** Many plans include a charge for each incoming and outgoing message (although some plans only charge one way, usually incoming). This might be as little as ten cents a message, but it could be fifteen or twenty cents a message.

- **Your provider sets a monthly message limit.** Some plans include a maximum number of messages per month (incoming or outgoing, but usually both) for a monthly fee. For example, you might get 300 messages for $5 a month. If you exceed that limit, a per-message charge applies.

- **Your provider gives you unlimited messages.** Almost all mobile providers offer unlimited plans for a monthly fee, typically around $15 a month.

Check with your provider to see what text messaging plan you have, and consider adjusting the plan to match your expected Twitter usage. Obviously, if you're lucky enough to have unlimited text messaging, then you have no worries either sending or receiving Twitter updates on your phone. However, if you have to worry about per-message fees or monthly limits, then give this whole Twitter-on-your-mobile-phone thing some thought based on the tweeting patterns of you and your friends:

- **Sending tweets — you tweet only once in a while.** If you just post updates once or twice a day, then you won't run up exorbitant per-message charges or bump up against your monthly ceiling, so go ahead and Twitter away.

- **Sending tweets — you tweet frequently.** If you regularly post a dozen times a day or more, then you're either looking at monthly per-message fees totaling $30 or $40 or more, or you're looking at total monthly messages in the 300 to 400 range, or more. In this case, you probably want to consider the SMS alternatives I run through in the next section.

- **Receiving tweets.** Even if you only follow a few people, you're likely to receive hundreds of messages per month, and if you follow a few dozen people or more, then you're well into thousands of messages each month. For many tweeters, receiving updates on your mobile phone is only practical if you have an unlimited text messaging plan.

Non-SMS Twitter alternatives

If you don't have text messaging on your mobile phone rate plan, or if you've done your calculations and it looks like your Twitter habit would put you in the poorhouse within months, does that mean the tweet-on-the-go world is out of reach? Not at all! You've actually got several alternate routes to mobile Twittering:

- Use the version of Twitter's site designed for mobile Web browsers.

- Send your tweets via e-mail (yes, there's a trick to doing this).

- If your phone has a data plan and a Web browser, use one of the Web sites designed for mobile Twitter use, such as Hahlo.com.

- If you can add applications to your phone, install a Twitter mobile phone client such as Twitterific or TwitterBerry.

All of these techniques are explored in this chapter.

Twitter's phone numbers

Once your phone is activated on Twitter (as described in the next section), you text updates and other commands to a special Twitter phone number. The number you use depends on where you live:

- **United States.** Use the short code number 40404.

- **Canada.** Use the short code number 21212.

- **Britain.** Use the short code number 86444.

- **Germany.** Use the long code number +49 17 6888 50505.

- **Sweden.** Use the long code number +46 737 494222.

- **Elsewhere.** Use the long code number +44 7624 801423.

Twitter is quite strict with these numbers, meaning that, for example, if you live in the U.S., you must use the 40404 short code, and if you live somewhere other than the U.S, Canada, Britain, Germany, or Sweden, you must use the general international long code (+44 7624 801423). If you fall within the latter camp, be sure to check your rate plan very carefully for two things:

- Does your provider consider the number +44 7624 801423 to be an international call?

- If so, find out what it will charge you for each international message (it could be quite a lot).

As I write this, Twitter will only send updates and other messages to Bell Mobility customers in Canada and Vodafone customers in Great Britain, and it won't send any messages to your phone if you use the general international code (+44 7624 801423). However, you can send messages to Twitter if you use any other Canadian provider, or if you use the general international code.

Activating Your Mobile Phone

Your first step toward using your phone with Twitter is to activate the phone in your Twitter account. Basically, you let Twitter know your phone number, and it then provides you with a code that you text to Twitter to confirm. Here are the specific steps:

1. **Sign in to your Twitter account.**

2. **Click Settings.** Your account settings appear.

3. **Click the Devices tab.**

4. **Type your mobile phone number in the text box.** On most systems this text box is indistinguishable from the page background, so see figure 5.1 for its location. Precede the number with a plus sign (+) and be sure to include your country code.

5.1 Use the Devices tab to type your mobile phone number.

5. **Select the It's okay for Twitter to send txt messages to my phone check box.**

6. **Click Save.** Twitter displays a code and tells you to text it to your local Twitter phone number.

7. **On your mobile phone, access the SMS feature, start a new message, type your local Twitter phone number, enter the code supplied by Twitter, and then send the message.**

Within a minute or two, Twitter sends you the return message shown in figure 5.2.

The next time you load the Devices tab in your Twitter settings, you see the configuration shown in figure 5.3. I discuss the new controls as you work through this chapter. For now, you're ready to starting sending updates through your phone!

✉ 21212

19 Mar 2009 22:25:22

1/2: Twitter has verified your device and sms alerts are enabled. Std msg charges apply. Send 'off' to silence or 'stop' to quit. Send '

5.2 Twitter sends you the message shown here when it has verified your mobile phone.

Paul

| Account | Password | Devices | Notices | Picture | Design |

Note: In Canada we currently only send SMSes to Bell Mobility subscribers.

Mobile Phone: +13175556789
Device updates:
On ⏷ PIN (optional): Save

(Send updates to: 21212)

Sleep:
☐ Turn off updates during these hours
midnight ⏷ to midnight ⏷ Save

Delete and start over?

5.3 With your mobile phone verified, the Devices tab now looks like the version shown here.

Notice in figure 5.3 that the Device updates setting is set to On by default. Don't be alarmed, however; that setting does *not* mean that you'll soon be inundated with your friend's tweets. Twitter turns off device updates for all the people you follow, so you won't see any incoming tweets until you turn on device updates for some friends. See the section "Receive a person's updates on your mobile phone" later in this chapter.

Sending an Update from Your Mobile Phone

Once your mobile phone is verified with Twitter, your phone becomes just another Twitter tool that you can use to post updates, send replies, fire off direct messages, and much more. The next few sections provide the details.

Sending an update from your mobile phone as text

The next time you're out and about without a computer in range and a perfectly tweetable thought, idea, or sight comes your way, pull out your trusty mobile phone and perform these almost-too-simple-to-be-true steps to post your update:

1. **On your mobile phone, access the SMS feature, and then start a new message.**

2. **Use the phone's text messaging interface to specify that you want the text sent to the Twitter phone number for your locale.**

3. **Type your message.** Figure 5.4 shows an example. Notice that the SMS application on my BlackBerry tells me how many characters I have left before I hit 140 in the bar at the top. *Very* sweet.

5.4 Address your message to your local Twitter phone number and then type your tweet text.

4. **Send the message.** Your phone shoots the message to Twitter, and it then appears on your timeline, usually within a few seconds, as shown in figure 5.5.

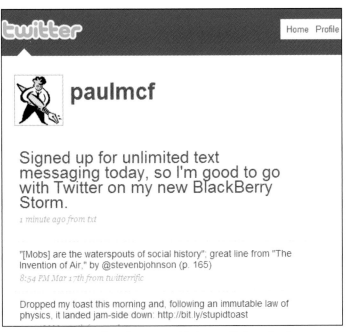

5.5 The text message from figure 5.4 added to my Twitter timeline

Sending an update using Twitter's mobile Web site

There are lots of third-party tools you can use to manage your Twitter account using your mobile phone, and you learn about many of them later in this chapter. And you've seen that you can also use your phone's SMS feature to send tweets. However, what if you don't want to install a Twitter application on your phone, or if your phone doesn't support third-party programs? Or what if your mobile phone plan doesn't include text messaging, or it charges big-time fees for each message?

If your phone includes a mobile Web browser and you've got a data plan, then you can work around each of these problems by using Twitter's mobile Web site to send your tweets. This site is optimized for the small screens that are typical of mobile phones, so you can tweet to your heart's content while you're on the go.

Here are the steps to follow:

1. **Point your mobile Web browser to http://m.twitter.com/.** Twitter redirects the browser to the mobile login page.

2. **Use the Username text box to enter your Twitter username.**

3. **Use the Password text box to enter your Twitter password.**

4. **Select Sign In.** Twitter takes you to your home page, which appears something like the screen shown in figure 5.6.

5. **Type your update text in the What are you doing? box.**

6. **Choose Update.** Twitter sends your update.

7. **Scroll down to the bottom of the page and click Sign Out.** Twitter logs you out of your account.

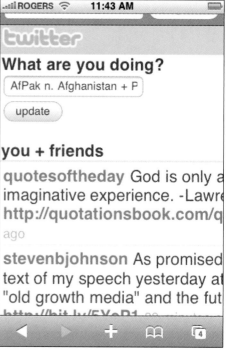

5.6 You can use Twitter's mobile Web site to post an update from your mobile phone or PDA.

Twitter's mobile Web site doesn't have the handy character countdown to let you know how much room you have left in your tweet. However, the text box accepts a maximum of 140 characters, so if you find you can't type anything else in the box, then it means you've hit the max.

Sending an update from your mobile phone as e-mail

If you don't want to tweet via SMS (because you don't have a text messaging plan or the plan you've got is not Twitter-friendly) and you can't use the Twitter mobile site (say, because you don't have a data plan), it's still possible to post updates by phone (although not to receive updates). The trick here is a bit convoluted, but it works. What you're going to do is take advantage of two different features that are available from various services on the Web:

- **E-mail-to-blog.** This is a feature that provides you with a special e-mail address, and any messages you send to that address are automatically posted to your blog. Blog hosts such as Blogger, TypePad, and WordPress support this feature.

- **Blog feed-to-Twitter.** This is a feature that monitors your blog's RSS feed and automatically sends new posts to your Twitter account. Services such as Twitterfeed and Tweet Later offer this feature.

In other words, your tweet by e-mail process works like this:

1. Use your mobile phone to send an e-mail message to your blog's e-mail address.

2. Your blog host posts that message to your blog.

3. Your Twitter application detects the new post via your blog's RSS feed.

4. Your Twitter application sends the post text as an update to your Twitter account.

Like I said, it's a bit of a circuitous route, but it doesn't take all that long to set up, and once it's running you never have to give it a second thought.

So your first chore is to set up and configure a blog on a host that offers the e-mail-to-blog feature. Here are some options:

- **Blogger.** Go to www.blogger.com and create a new blog (it's free). Click the Settings tab, click Email, add text to the Email Posting Address text box to complete your posting address, and then click Save Settings.

- **TypePad.** Go to www.typepad.com and create a new blog (plans start at $4.95 a month). Click your blog, click the Configure tab, click Mobile, and then make a note of the Secret Address.

- **WordPress.** You need to be using the full version of WordPress available from http://wordpress.org (the free version at http://wordpress.com doesn't offer the Post via E-mail feature) or sign up for a WordPress blog host. See the instructions at http://codex.wordpress.org/Blog_by_Email.

- **LiveJournal.** Go to www.livejournal.com and create a free blog. Click the Account link, and then click the Mobile tab. In the Email Posting section, fill in an address and a PIN number, and then click Save.

- **Windows Live Spaces.** Create a free blog at http://spaces.live.com. In your space, choose Options ⇨ More options, click Spaces, and then click E-mail publishing. Select the Turn on e-mail publishing check box, fill in the fields, and then click Save.

Be sure to guard the e-mail address you use for posting to your blog. Otherwise, anyone who knows the address can post to your blog, and therefore also to your Twitter account!

note The tweet uses the format *Subject*: *Body*, where *Subject* is the e-mail message subject line, and *Body* is the e-mail text.

With your blog host's e-mail-to-blog feature set up, the next step is to get your blog's feed into Twitter. Here are two services to check out:

- **Twitterfeed** (http://twitterfeed.com). This site forwards blog feeds to Twitter and other sites. See Chapter 9 to learn how to add your blog feed to this site.

- **Tweet Later** (http://tweetlater.com). This site offers a smorgasbord of Twitter features. The free version doesn't offer an RSS-to-Twitter feature, but the Professional version does (although it costs about $20 per month, so it's a bit steep just for this).

Now you're good to go. Use your mobile phone to fire off an e-mail message to your blog host's e-mail-to-blog address, as shown in figure 5.7. After a while (it depends on how frequently you set up Twitterfeed to check for fresh posts), your message shows up as a tweet on your Twitter account, as shown in figure 5.8.

5.7 Use your phone's e-mail application to send the tweet text to your blog host's e-mail-to-blog address.

 note If you use Twitterfeed, be sure to deselect the Include item link check box in the feed settings. Otherwise, your tweet includes a link to your blog "post," which is not what you want.

paulmcf

Hey!: Figured out a cool way to send tweets via email. Read all about it in my forthcoming Twitter book.

less than a minute ago from twitterfeed

Loved this letter: "A newspaper is to inform and also educate. The written word, especially in a newspaper, should be used correctly."

about 5 hours ago from TweetDeck

5.8 The e-mail message is eventually forwarded as an update on your Twitter account.

Configuring Twitter to nudge you for updates

If you get busy with a project or some other time-draining commitment, you might forget to keep up your end of the Twitter conversation. Hey, it happens. If you don't want your account to get stale and you want to avoid your mutual followers nudging you (as described in Chapter 4), then you can get Twitter to do the nudging by sending you a reminder to post. This reminder gets sent to your mobile phone, so you'll get it no matter where you are (assuming your phone is on, of course).

This feature is called Auto Nudge, and Twitter fires off the reminder message any time you haven't posted for 24 hours. Follow these steps to configure Auto Nudge on your account:

1. **Sign in to your Twitter account.**

2. **Click Settings.** Your account settings appear.

3. **Click the Notices tab.**

4. **Select the Auto Nudge check box, as shown in figure 5.9.**

5. **Click Save.** Twitter saves the new setting and will nudge you the moment you start to slack off.

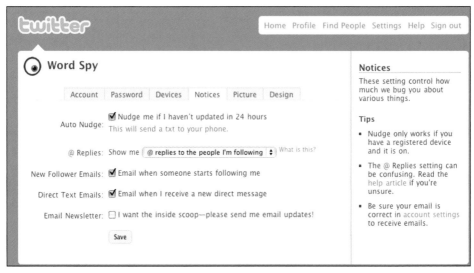

5.9 Select the Auto Nudge check box to have Twitter send an electronic poke in the ribs whenever you have not tweeted in 24 hours.

Sending a reply from your mobile phone

Replies are open to anyone whose account isn't protected, so you can reply to *any* Twitter user from your phone. This is great if you want to send a witty retort while you're out and about. Here's how it's done:

1. **On your mobile phone, access the SMS feature and start a new message.**

2. **Enter the Twitter phone number for your locale.**

3. **Type @ followed by the Twitter username of the person you want to reply to.** Be sure to add at least one space after the username.

4. **Type the rest of your message.** Figure 5.10 shows an example reply.

5. **Send the message.** Your phone hands the message off to Twitter, and it then appears on your timeline, usually within a few seconds, as shown in figure 5.11.

5.10 To reply, send a message that begins with @*username* to your local Twitter phone number.

paulmcf

@muckp I added your "followworthy" coinage to the Twictionary http://bit.ly/glAl #neologism

8 minutes ago from txt

Hey!: Figured out a cool way to send tweets via email. Read all about it in my forthcoming Twitter book.
36 minutes ago from twitterfeed

5.11 The reply message from figure 5.10 added to my Twitter timeline

Sending a direct message from your mobile phone

If you're in a mutual-follow Twitter connection with someone, you can drop that person a direct message. If you happen to be running around town or stuck in a meeting and you think of something you want to tell your friend directly, you can post the direct message right from your mobile phone. Here are the steps to follow:

1. **On your mobile phone, access the SMS feature, and then start a new message.**

2. **Type the Twitter phone number for your locale.**

3. **Type d followed by the Twitter username of the person you want to direct message.** Be sure to add at least one space after the username.

4. **Type the rest of your message.** Figure 5.12 shows an example direct message.

5.12 To send a direct message, send a text that begins with d *username*.

5. **Send the message.** Your phone sends the message, and before too long it appears in that person's Direct Messages timeline, as shown in figure 5.13.

Send [▼] a direct message.   140   (●) wordspy

785 | 800 | 123
following | followers | updates

Twit·ter Search
n. a service for discovering
what's happening right now.

send

Inbox   Sent

Direct Messages Sent Only to You

paulmcf Call me when you get a chance: 317-555-4321.
Thanks!
5 minutes ago

Home

@Replies

Direct Messages   44

5.13 The direct message from figure 5.12 added to the user's Direct Messages timeline

Protecting your updates with a PIN number

The malicious hackers of the world are, to be charitable, a resourceful bunch, and it seems there's no service in the world they haven't cracked. That includes SMS, where there are now tools available online that enable evildoers to spoof SMS messages as long as they know the mobile number of the person being duped.

To guard against such attacks, Twitter offers a security feature called a PIN (personal identification number), which is a four-digit number that (ideally) only you know. When you add a PIN to your Twitter account, you can only post an update from your mobile phone if that text message begins with your four-digit PIN. No PIN, no post.

If you're concerned about SMS spoofing (and while it's not a huge deal right now, it could easily become a problem one of these days), follow these steps to protect your mobile updates:

1. **Sign in to your Twitter account.**

2. **Click Settings.** Your account settings appear.

3. **Click the Devices tab.**

4. **Type a four-digit number in the PIN text box.** On most systems this text box is indistinguishable from the page background, so see figure 5.14 for its location.

5. **Click Save.** Twitter saves the new setting, and you must now precede all mobile phone messages with your PIN.

Paul McFedries

Account	Password	Devices	Notices	Picture	Design

Note: In Canada we currently only send SMSes to Bell Mobility subscribers.

Mobile Phone: +13175556789
Device updates:

On ▼   PIN (optional): 1234   [Save]

(Send updates to: 21212)

Sleep:
☐ Turn off updates during these hours

[midnight ▼] to [midnight ▼]   [Save]

[Delete and start over?]

5.14 To prevent SMS spoofing, add a four-digit PIN to your Twitter account.

Following Twitterers on Your Mobile Phone

Although most Twitterers use their mobile phones to send tweets, replies, and direct messages, you can also use mobile text messages to handle various following and friend chores: follow new people, stop following people, send nudges, receive a friend's updates and direct messages, get a person's Twitter profile, and much more. The next few sections take you through the details.

Following a person from your mobile phone

So you're at a cocktail party and you mention that your favorite writer is Steven Johnson (author of *Everything Bad Is Good for You*, among others), and someone tells you that he has a Twitter account and this person even knows his username: stevenbjohnson. That's not hard to remember, but you know that if you don't do something right away, you'll forget to follow your literary hero. Fortunately, you can pull out your trusty mobile phone and immediately update your Twitter account to follow him. Nice! Here's how it's done:

1. **Open your mobile phone's SMS feature and start a new message.**

2. **Type the Twitter phone number for your location.**

3. **Type** FOLLOW.

Twitter's text commands aren't case sensitive, so it doesn't matter if you use FOLLOW or follow (or even FoLlOw, for that matter).

4. **Type a space and then the Twitter username of the person you want to follow.** Figure 5.15 shows an example follow command.

5. **Send the message.** When Twitter receives the command, it updates your friend list to include the user.

 It's not possible to stop following a person from your mobile phone. To stop following someone, you have to use the Twitter Web site.

Receiving a person's updates on your mobile phone

When you first activate your mobile phone with Twitter, it turns on the device notifications setting, which means that you've authorized Twitter to send you stuff. At first, this just means you receive the following:

```
              119
To: 21212
Follow stevenbjohnson
```

5.15 To follow a user, send a text with follow *username.*

- **Results of commands you've sent.** For example, if you send follow *username* to start following someone, Twitter sends you a message in return to acknowledge that you're now following that person.

- **Direct messages sent to you.** These could be direct messages sent from people you follow (and who follow you), or the results of a command you sent to a Twitter bot.

If you also want to get the tweets posted by someone you follow delivered to your mobile phone, then you must activate device updates for that person. Twitter gives you various ways to do this, depending on where you are in the Twitter interface:

- **In the list of people you follow:** Each user has a Device updates setting, which is initially set to Off. Select the On option to get updates from that person.

- **On a person's profile page:** Click the Following link to open the person's follow options, and then select the On option under Device updates, as shown in figure 5.16.

⦿ **On your mobile phone:** Text the command ON *username*, where *username* is the Twitter screen name of the person whose updates you want on your phone.

There may be users for whom you don't want to see every tweet on your phone, just the occasional one. In that case, leave that person's Device updates setting on Off. To retrieve the latest update from that person, use your phone to text the command GET *username*, where *username* is the person's Twitter screen name.

5.16 To receive a person's updates on your mobile phone, select the On option under Device updates.

Nudging a person from your mobile phone

Haven't heard from one of your friends in a while? Give him or her a nudge from your mobile phone:

1. **Launch SMS on your mobile phone and start a new message.**

2. **Type your Twitter phone number.**

3. **Type** NUDGE. Remember that it is not case sensitive.

4. **Type a space and then the Twitter username of the person you want to nudge.**

5. **Send the message.** Twitter sends a nudge message to your friend. The message looks like this (where *yourname* is your Twitter username):

```
yourname nudged you to update Twitter.
Do that by replying to this message!
```

Marking an update as a favorite from your mobile phone

Once you start getting updates on your mobile phone, you never know when a particularly good tweet might come your way. In fact, you might receive a tweet that's so good you want to add it to your Favorites timeline. How can you do that without a Web browser? Use your phone, of course! Here's how:

1. **Start your phone's SMS tool and launch a new message.**

2. **Type your location's Twitter phone number.**

3. **Type** FAV.

4. **Type a space and then the Twitter username of the person whose tweet you want to favorite.**

5. **Send the message.** Twitter adds the user's most recent message to your Favorites timeline and sends you back a confirmation message.

Twitter favorites the most recent tweet by the user, so if you're dealing with a prolific tweeter, be sure to text the FAV command as soon as possible.

Retrieving a profile on your mobile phone

When you're on the Twitter Web site you can view a person's profile page to find out a bit about them: name, location, Web site, and one-line bio. If you need the same information while away from Twitter, you can use your mobile phone to retrieve it. Follow these steps:

1. **Open the SMS application on your phone and start a new message.**

2. **Type your Twitter phone number.**

3. **Type** WHOIS.

4. **Type a space and then the username of the person you're curious about.**

5. **Send the message.** Twitter returns a text message with the user's profile information, as shown in figure 5.17.

5.17 Text WHOIS *username* to receive the profile information of a Twitter user.

Stopping a person's updates on your mobile phone

If you're receiving a person's tweets on your mobile phone, you may find that the updates aren't as good as you thought, or can wait until the next time you're online. Similarly, you might have turned on Device updates for a few too many friends, and now your mobile phone's SMS inbox is stuffed. Either way, you might want to stop a person's update from going to your phone, and once again Twitter gives you multiple methods. The one you choose depends on where you're located in the Twitterverse:

- **In the list of people you follow:** Locate the Devices updates setting for the person you want to stop receiving tweets from, and select the Off option.

- **On a person's profile page:** Click the Following link to open the person's follow options, and then select the Off option under Device updates.

- **On your mobile phone:** Text the command OFF *username*, where *username* is the Twitter screen name of the person whose updates you no longer require.

Receiving only direct messages on your mobile phone

For many tweeters, their friend timeline is something they watch with varying degrees of interest, particularly if they follow dozens of hundreds of people. For these users, the real meat of their Twitter experience lies in the direct messages they receive from mutual friends. If you fall into this camp, then you might want to configure your account device settings to send only direct messages to your mobile phone. Here's how:

1. **Sign in to your Twitter account.**
2. **Click Settings.** Your account settings appear.
3. **Click the Devices tab.**
4. **Use the Device updates list to choose Direct Messages, as shown in figure 5.18.**
5. **Click Save.** Twitter saves the new setting, and now only sends direct messages to your mobile phone.

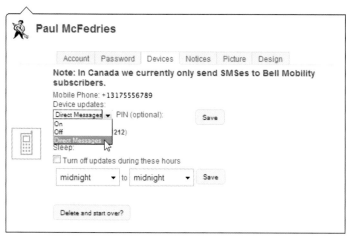

5.18 In the Device updates list, choose Direct Messages to have only direct messages sent to your phone.

Stopping all updates on your mobile phone

If you've activated Device updates for a number of your friends, you might start feeling a bit overwhelmed if they start tossing dozens of tweets a day at your phone. If you want to take a break and catch up, don't go through the hassle of turning off Device updates for every person. Instead, you can tell Twitter to stop sending you any updates. You can do this either on the Twitter site or using your phone.

Follow these steps to turn off Device updates using the Twitter Web site:

1. **Sign in to your Twitter account.**

2. **Click Settings.** Your account settings appear.

3. **Click the Devices tab.**

4. **Use the Device updates list to choose Off.**

5. **Click Save.** Twitter saves the new setting and no longer sends any Device updates to your mobile phone.

 When you're ready to resume updates (and direct messages, if you turned those off too), simply open your settings on the Twitter site and choose On in the Device updates list or, from your mobile phone, text the command ON to your local Twitter number.

Here are the steps to follow to turn off Device updates from your mobile phone:

1. **Start the SMS tool on your phone and begin a new message.**

2. **Type the Twitter phone number for your locale.**

3. **Type** OFF.

4. **Send the message.** Twitter turns off Device updates and sends you a confirmation message.

If you also want to prevent Twitter from sending direct messages to your mobile phone, wait until you get the response from Twitter for the OFF command, then text a second OFF command to your local Twitter number.

Sending a Twitter invitation from your mobile phone

Although it's still loads of fun to follow complete strangers on Twitter (assuming, of course, that those strangers have the mental wherewithal to be interesting or at least fun), Twitter's appeal grows exponentially with each new real-world friend you can follow. If you know of someone who's not currently on Twitter, but you'd like her to be, then you can use your mobile phone to extend a Twitter invitation to that person's mobile phone. Give it a whirl:

1. **Fire up your mobile phone's SMS application and start a new message.**

2. **Type your Twitter phone number.**

3. **Type** INVITE.

4. **Type a space and then the mobile phone number of the person you're inviting.**

5. **Send the message.** Twitter sends an invitation SMS message to your friend's mobile phone. The message looks like this (where *yourname* is your Twitter username):

```
yourname invited you to Twitter! Reply with your
name to start. Standard message charges apply, send
'stop' to quit. help@twitter.com for help.
```

Getting your Twitter stats on your mobile phone

Want a quick update on the number of people who are following you and the number of people you're following? Easier done than said, because you can get that data sent right to your phone. Here's how:

1. **Use your mobile phone's SMS application to begin a new message.**
2. **Type your Twitter phone number.**
3. **Type** STATS.
4. **Send the message.** Twitter texts you back a message with your follower and following numbers.

A Summary of Twitter's Text Commands

I've gone through quite a few text commands in this chapter, so now's a good time to pause and take in the bird's-eye view of things. Table 5.1 presents a list of all the text commands you can use from your mobile phone.

Table 5.1 Twitter's Text Commands

Command	What It Does
message	Posts *message* as a tweet.
@*username message*	Sends a reply to *username*.
D *username message*	Sends a direct message to *username*.
FOLLOW *username*	Configures your Twitter profile to follow *username*.
NUDGE *username*	Sends a message to *username* asking them to tweet something soon.
FAV *username*	Marks *username*'s most recent tweet as a favorite.
WHOIS *username*	Returns the profile information for *username*.
ON *username*	Turns on Device updates for *username*.
OFF *username*	Turns off Device updates for *username*. (You can also use the LEAVE command.)
GET *username*	Returns the most recent tweet posted by *username*.
OFF	Turns off Device updates for all users. Send OFF again to also turn off direct messages.
ON	Turns on Device updates and direct messages.
STOP	Stops Twitter from sending all messages to your phone immediately. (You can also use the QUIT command.)
INVITE *phone number*	Sends an SMS invitation to a friend's mobile *phone number*.
STATS	Returns your number of followers, how many people you're following, and which words you're tracking.

You can also use the commands in Table 5.1 in the Twitter Web site (for example, in the What are you doing? text box) as well as in most Twitter clients.

Tools for Managing Twitter from Your Mobile Phone

Once you've done the Twitter thing on your mobile phone for a while, you realize that it has its pros and cons:

- On the pro side, it's fantastic to be able to post, reply, and send direct messages wherever you happen to be, to follow folks right away, and to see updates in real-time.

- On the con side, the command-line style interface leaves something to be desired. The Twitter Web site is nice because it comes with little icons and controls that you can simply click to send @replies, favorite a tweet, get a user's profile, and more.

Wouldn't it be great if you could somehow combine the immediacy of a mobile phone with the convenience of the Twitter site? Yes, it certainly would. Happily, other people with more programming skills than you or I have thought of this, too, and they've gone and done something about it. A couple of things, actually:

- **Applications.** There are now several Twitter client applications available that you can install on your mobile phone (if your phone supports that kind of thing).

- **Web sites.** There are also a number of Twitter-focused Web sites available that are optimized for mobile phones (if your phone has a mobile Web browser and you've got a data plan from your provider).

In both cases, you get immediacy because you're managing your Twitter account from a mobile device, but you also get convenience because the applications and sites offer snazzy interfaces that make it easy to perform most common Twitter tasks. The rest of this chapter takes you through a few of these tools so you can get an idea what's out there.

The collection of applications and Web sites that I list here isn't even remotely comprehensive. If you want more, the best place to go is the Mobile Apps sections of the Twitter Fan Wiki: http://twitter.pbwiki.com/Apps#Mobileapps.

Mobile phone applications for Twitter

If your mobile phone supports third-party applications, then installing a Twitter client program is a great way to go because the program works anywhere you have a data connection, whether it's on the cellular network or via a network connection such as Wi-Fi or Bluetooth. The next few sections take quick looks at a few interesting Twitter programs.

I'm assuming here that you know how to install applications on your mobile phone. See your manual if all this is new to you.

note

TwitterBerry

TwitterBerry is a nice Twitter client that runs on most BlackBerry devices, including the Storm, Bold, Curve, and Pearl. TwitterBerry is free, and you can download it from www.orangetame.com/ota/twitterberry/.

When you first start TwitterBerry, the program asks for your Twitter username and password, and presents you with a few options, as shown in figure 5.19. Enter your username and password, adjust the settings, if necessary (the defaults are fine for now), and then select Test Connection to make sure TwitterBerry can properly connect to your Twitter account. Select back to return to the application.

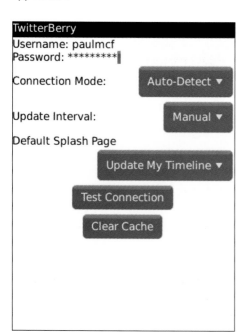

5.19 When you first start TwitterBerry, you see this settings screen.

The main TwitterBerry screen (what it calls the splash screen) offers the classic Twitter "What are you doing?" prompt, as shown in figure 5.20. You enter your update message in the text box (a Characters Available line counts down to 0), then you open the menu and choose Update to post your tweet.

5.20 You use TwitterBerry's default screen to post tweets.

The TwitterBerry developer does offer a PayPal donation link, and if you decide to use TwitterBerry full-time, please consider passing along whatever you can afford.

You use the menu to switch from one TwitterBerry screen to another:

- **Friends Timeline.** This shows a list of the tweets posted by the people you follow (see figure 5.21). Select or open a tweet and the menu then sprouts related commands such as Reply, Direct Message, and Favorite.

- **Get Replies.** Displays the replies people have sent you.

- **Direct Messages.** Displays the direct messages people have sent you.

- **Public Timeline.** Shows Twitter's public timeline (tweets from all nonprotected accounts).

- **My Timeline.** Displays the tweets you've posted.

- **Get Friends List.** Retrieves the list of people you follow.

- **Sent Direct Messages.** Displays the direct messages you've sent.

- **Configure.** Returns you to the settings page.

What You and Your Friends Are Doing

TheOnion
In Focus: Spring-Cleaning Tips http://bit.ly/116...
less than a minute ago

cshirky
RT @PerpetuumZg That's what your blog's fo...
5 minutes ago

TheOnion
BREAKING: Obama On Special Olympics Gaff...
18 minutes ago

quotesnack
Thought is the seed of action, but action is as...
29 minutes ago

quotesnack
Self-sacrifice is the real miracle out of which...
30 minutes ago

quotesoftheday
I know by my own pot how the others boil. -P...
31 minutes ago

Wordola Wordola
Wordola Players at Tweetizen: http://tinyurl.c...
41 minutes ago

cshirky
RT @joshmishell: @cshirky if it doesn't fit in...
about an hour ago

cshirky
RT @sevensixfive @cshirky how are distingui...
about an hour ago

5.21 TwitterBerry's Friends Timeline command displays the tweets posted by the folks you follow.

TinyTwitter

TinyTwitter is a neat little program that packs a lot of features into its tiny frame. It has a Java version that should work on any BlackBerry as well as any phone that supports Java applications, and a separate version that works on Windows Mobile-based PocketPCs and Smartphones. Navigate to www.tinytwitter.com to download it for free.

When you first start the program you're prompted for your Twitter credentials. Enter your username and password, and then choose Done from the menu to sign in to your Twitter account. By default, TinyTwitter displays your friend timeline, as shown in figure 5.22. Select a tweet to read it.

TinyTwitter's menu is crammed with useful commands:

nytimes: Your Money: A Layoff Survivor's Duty to the Less Fortunate http://tinyurl.com/dd2u75
5m 14s ago web

TinyTwitter: Welcome to Tiny Twitter

TinyTwitter: Here are some shortcuts

BJMendelson: *ask Google. Holy typo.

iamdiddy: New Crazy Joint/Bad Boy

BJMendelson: Now if only I can

garyvee: my bracket looks like my

google: Spring is here! Temperatures

alleyinsider: Dell Phone "Back To The

someecards: topics to avoid with laid

markhoppus: Conference call about

brookeburke: marinating my meat,

Agent_M: Oooh, and now a recently

TIME: THE PAGE: Obamas to Camp

5.22 TinyTwitter shows your friend timeline initially.

- **Update.** Refreshes the current timeline.

- **Tweet.** Displays a text box so you can send an update.

- **Access Links.** Displays the links that appear in the highlighted tweet.

- **Reply.** Sends a reply to the person who sent the highlighted tweet.

- **Reply All.** Sends a reply to the person who sent the highlighted tweet, as well as every other Twitter username included in the tweet.

- **Direct.** Sends a direct message to the person who sent the highlighted tweet.

- **Favorite.** Marks the highlighted tweet as a favorite.

- **Retweets.** Retweets the highlighted tweet.

- **User Timeline.** Returns the list of tweets posted by the person who sent the highlighted tweet.

- **Unfollow.** Stops following the highlighted user.

- **Delete.** Deletes the highlighted tweet.

- **Delete All.** Deletes all the tweets.

- **Inbox.** Displays the replies and direct messages people have sent you.

- **Nearby Twitter Peeps.** Looks for users who are near your location (if your phone supports GPS).

- **Search.** Lets you search Twitter.

- **What's Hot.** Displays the latest Twitter trends.

- **Public Timeline.** Shows Twitter's public timeline (tweets from all nonprotected accounts).

- **Hide Friends.** Enables you to hide the tweets from selected friends.

- **Credentials.** Enables you to change your Twitter account username and password.

Twitterific

If you use an iPhone (or an iPod touch) and your needs are simple, give the Twitterific client a test drive. The App Store offers a free version that displays ads within your timelines, as well as Twitterific Premium, an ad-free version that costs $9.99. Once it's downloaded and installed, tap the new Twitterific icon. The program displays the public timeline initially, so tap Setup to enter your Twitter username and password, and Twitterific immediately downloads your friend timeline, as shown in figure 5.23.

Double-tap a tweet to open it. This displays a larger version of the tweet for easier reading, and you can see in figure 5.24 that you have several tweet-related icons at your disposal: Reply, Favorite, and User Info. Tap List View to return to the timeline.

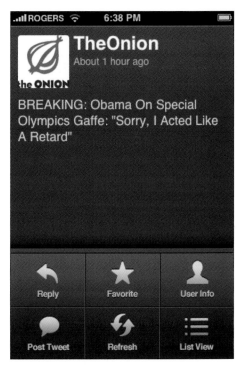

5.23 A friend timeline displayed in the free version of Twitterific (notice the ad)

5.24 Open a tweet to read it and access the tweet commands.

Twittelator Pro

If you're more of a Twitter power user with an iPhone (or iPod touch), consider loading Twittelator Pro onto your iPhone. This powerful application (available from the App Store for $4.99) does just about everything a Twitter client should (and more!), and all with a nice interface to boot. After you start the program and enter your Twitter account credentials, Twittelator Pro displays your friend timeline, as shown in figure 5.25.

You use the icons in the toolbar at the bottom of the screen to switch from one section of the program to another: Replies, Messages, Settings, and More, which displays a long list of really useful Twitter tools: Search, Mine (your tweets), My Msgs (your replies and directs), Subgroups, Trends, Everyone, Stocks, Recents, Bookmarks, Favorites, Log, and Misc. There's plenty here to keep you busy for a long time.

To work with a tweet, tap and hold the tweet text for a couple of seconds, and you then see a screen that looks like the one shown in figure 5.26. This is a power-users dream, with icons for replying, sending a direct message, retweeting, e-mailing, copying, and favoriting the tweet, as well as for copying the tweet link, if it has one.

5.25 The friend timeline in Twittelator Pro

5.26 Tap and hold a tweet to see a satisfyingly large number of tweet options.

Twittelator Pro also supports multiple Twitter accounts, which is a gotta-have-it feature if, like me, you manage multiple Twitter identities.

More mobile phone applications

The perfect mobile Twitter application is a kind of Holy Grail for gadget-obsessed tweeters, one that they seek constantly but fear they'll never find. If you're on the same quest, here are a few other applications to consider:

- **Blackbird.** This is a basic Twitter client for BlackBerry mobile phones. See http://dossy. org/twitter/blackbird/.

- **ceTwit.** This is a full-featured Windows Mobile 6 client, available from www.kosertech. com/blog/?page_id=5.

- **Jitter.** This is a simple, functional, and free Twitter client that's Java-based, so it works on a wide variety of mobile phones. Get it here: www.getjar.com/products/9943/ JitterTwitterclient.

- **Pocketwit.** This is a nice Windows Mobile 6 (or later) application with an interesting interface. See http://code.google.com/p/pocketwit/.

- **Tweetie.** This is an iPhone (or iPod Touch) application that you can download from the App Store for $2.99. It looks much like Twittelator Pro, but it has fewer features.

- **Twidroid.** This is a full-featured application designed for Android mobile phones. See http://twidroid.com.

- **TwitToday.** This is a free Windows Mobile 5 (or later) widget that installs a Twitter text box on your Today screen, so you can quickly send a tweet. It's available from http:// dalelane.co.uk/page.php?id=1047.

- **Twobile.** This is a Windows Mobile 5 (or later) application that is free, but surprisingly full-featured. As I write this, Twobile only supports touch-screen phones. You can get it here: www.infinitumsoftware.com/twobile.

Mobile phone Web sites for Twitter

If your mobile phone doesn't support third-party applications, or you just don't want to load outside applications on your phone, you can still get full-featured Twitter goodness by heading out to the Web with your phone's mobile browser. Web sites optimized for mobile phone Twittering aren't as powerful as the best mobile applications, and they're slower by a long shot, but they're still way more friendly than SMS, and they're all more powerful and feature-filled than the humble Twitter mobile site at http://m.twitter.com.

Dabr

The Dabr site (http://dabr.co.uk/) takes the official Twitter mobile site idea and runs with it. That is, it takes the simple interface of m.twitter.com and bolts on useful tweeter-friendly features such as your friend timeline, lists of the replies and directs you've received, Twitter search, lists of your favorites, followers, and friends, the public Twitter timeline, and more.

Once you sign in to your account, you see the Dabr main page, which not only offers a tweet text box, just like m.twitter.com, but also your friend timeline, as shown in figure 5.27. This is a sensible setup because you get the two most important Twitter features right up front. You use the toolbar across the top of the page to switch features.

Hahlo

The Hahlo Web site (http://hahlo.com/) works best with the iPhone. The home page offers text boxes for your Twitter username and password, and once you're signed in you see Hahlo's version of your profile page, which includes all the standard Twitter profile info as well as your total number of friends, followers, favorites, and updates. Tap the With Friends tab to see your friend timeline, as shown in figure 5.28. For each tweet, you get clickable links, plus a Reply icon and a Favorite icon (but no retweet icon, unfortunately).

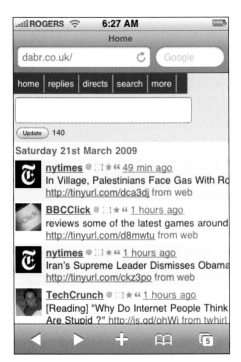

5.27 The Dabr main page shows your friend timeline and an update text box.

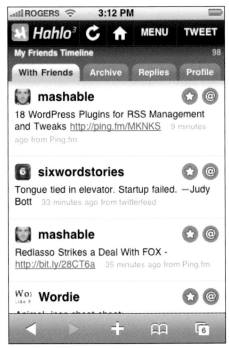

5.28 Tap the With Friends tab to see your friend timeline on the Hahlo mobile Web site.

The Profile tab isn't super useful as a home page, particularly because it's marred by an absurdly long welcome message. To configure Hahlo to load a different page at startup, scroll down the Profile page and tap Settings. Tap the Home Page list, tap the page you'd prefer to load initially (such as the Friends Timeline page), tap Done, and then tap Save.

Tap the Archive tab to see your update timeline, and tap the Replies tab to see the replies folks have sent you.

When you're ready to send an update, tap the TWEET icon in the upper-right corner of the screen. Hahlo presents you with a standard text box, and displays the number of characters you have left as you type (see figure 5.29).

Twitter power users will want to dive in to the many other features available on Hahlo, all of which you can see by tapping the MENU icon at the top of the screen. Hahlo pops up a window that contains a dozen icons that represent all of Hahlo's features, plus a sophisticated Search tool, as you can see in figure 5.30.

5.29 Tapping out a tweet using the Hahlo mobile Web site

5.30 Tap MENU to see this surprisingly long list of all Hahlo's other Twitter features.

PocketTweets

PocketTweets (http://pockettweets.com/) is another Twitter mobile site that's optimized for the iPhone. It's not as full-featured as Hahlo, but it offers a beautifully designed interface that's easy to use and handles all the basic Twitter tasks. Once you use the site to sign in to your Twitter account, you land on the home page, which presents your friend timeline, as shown in figure 5.31. For each tweet, PocketTweets includes clickable links, a Reply icon, and a Favorite icon (but, alas, no retweet icon).

When you get the urge to tweet something, tap the Update icon at the top of the page. PocketTweets loads the usual What are you doing? text box, although with a unique feature: As you type, it displays not only the number of characters you have left, but also the number of characters you've typed (see figure 5.32). I'm not sure why we need both numbers, but it's something a little different.

5.31 PocketTweets's gorgeous interface starts with your friend timeline on the home page.

5.32 PocketTweet's update text box tells you the number of characters you have left and the number of characters you've typed.

To get at the rest of the PocketTweets features, tap the Toolbar icon at the top of the page. This immediately whisks you to the bottom of the page, where you see the PocketTweets toolbar, as shown in figure 5.33. The toolbar includes icons that display your list of friends, replies, direct messages, and tweets, as well as Twitter's public timeline. Tap the Home icon to return to the top of the page.

More mobile phone sites for Twitter

To round out this look at Twitter Web sites that are mobile-friendly, here's a list of a few more sites that you can try:

- **Mobile Tweete.** http://m.tweete.net/
- **psychzzz.** http://mobi.psychzzz.com/
- **Slandr.** http://m.slandr.net/
- **Twitter2Go.** http://twitter2go.com

5.33 Tap the Toolbar icon to jump to the bottom of the home page, where the toolbar lives.

How Do I Find Stuff in Twitter?

1 2 3 4 5 **6** 7 8 9

Twitter users are clearly a talkative bunch, sending out roughly two million tweets every day (a number that will surely grow over time). The total number of tweets posted hit one billion in late 2008, a stat that at first blush seems intimidating, but with a bit of thought turns into an opportunity. After all, a billion updates represents a lot of information, much of it actually useful, so Twitter's database must be a goldmine of knowledge on almost any subject. But, how do you extract that gold? By taking advantage of Twitter's useful search engine, as well as the eyebrow-raisingly large collection of third-party Twitter search tools, as you see in this chapter.

Running a Basic Search

If you have a word or phrase that interests you and you'd like to see if your fellow Twitter users have been interested enough in the same term to tweet about it, the Twitter search engine can let you know. You can use it to search Twitter for a word, multiple words, or an exact phrase. Twitter takes your search text and looks for tweets that include matches in the tweet text or in the username of the tweeter.

You'd think getting to the Twitter search engine would be straightforward, but it's not, at least for many people. The problem is that, as I write this, Twitter is in the middle of testing a new interface that has quite a few differences from the old interface. To see what I mean, let's compare the home page sidebar in the two versions of the interface. First, check out the layout of the sidebar in the old version of Twitter, which appears in figure 6.1.

Then compare that with the layout of the sidebar as it appears in the new version of Twitter, as shown in figure 6.2.

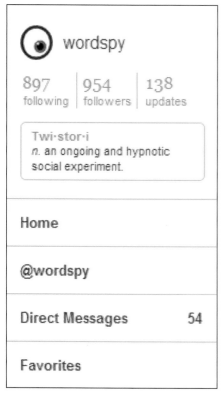

6.1 The sidebar in the old version of Twitter

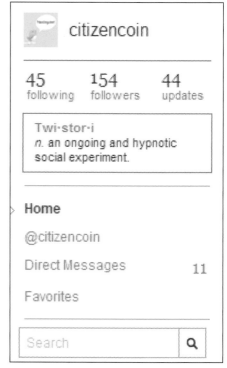

6.2 The sidebar in the new version of Twitter

The new sidebar is certainly cleaner and more attractive than the old one, but more to the point for our purposes, there is the obvious addition of a Search box right in the heart of the sidebar below the Favorites link. This is a huge and significant change because it makes searching Twitter absurdly easy. In the old interface, you have to scroll all the way down to the bottom of the page, pick out the Search link from the long horizontal list of links (see figure 6.3), and then click it. And the Twitter Search page you end up on isn't even technically on the same site as your profile, which leads to one of the biggest annoyances with the old version of Twitter search: there's no easy way to return to your Twitter account pages — the usual Home, Profile, and Settings links are gone. In the new interface, however, search is fully integrated into your Twitter home page: the Search box resides conveniently in the sidebar, and the search results appear on the home page in place of your friend timeline.

© 2009 Twitter   About Us   Contact   Blog   Status   Apps   API   Search   Help   Jobs   Terms   Privacy

6.3 In the old Twitter interface, you access the search engine by scrolling to the bottom of any Twitter page and clicking the Search link.

I expect that sometime in the near (I hope!) future Twitter will migrate everyone to the new interface, although as I write this no timeframe for that move has been announced. If you're still on the old interface, consider adding a bookmark or favorite for either the old Twitter Search page at http://search.twitter.com or the new Twitter Search page at http://twitter.com/search.

These differences reflect a new emphasis at Twitter on the importance of search. In the old interface, search was pretty much an afterthought, something bolted on because someone thought there ought to be some way to find tweets. Compare that with the new design where searching is fully integrated, which positions searching as a full and prominent member of the interface.

Not only is the way to get to the search feature different in the two versions, but they also use different search engines and return the search results differently. Because of these differences, I'll handle the two methods in separate sections.

Searching with the new Twitter interface

Because you'll certainly end up with the new Twitter interface eventually (if it's not already rolled out by the time you read this), I'll start with the new way of searching for tweets. In your Twitter home page, type your search term into the Search box, as shown in figure 6.4, and then press Enter or Return (or click the Search Twitter icon to the right of the box).

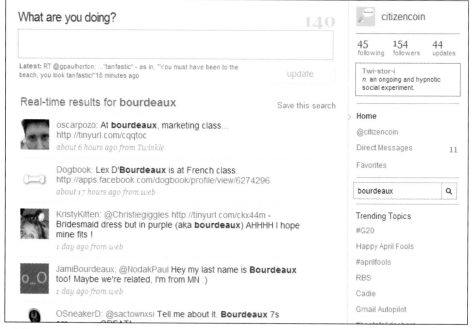

bourdeaux 🔍

6.4 In the new Twitter interface, type a search term in the Search text box.

Twitter then replaces your home page timeline with the search results, as shown in figure 6.5. The main part of the page shows the heading Real-time results for *term,* where *term* was the search word you entered. Below that you see a list of tweets that include your search term, ordered chronologically with the most recently posted tweet at the top.

6.5 The new Twitter search results appear on your Twitter home page and matching tweets appear in chronological order.

note

One of the nice features of the new search interface is that you can save searches for later use. If you have a frequently used search query, run the search and then click Save this search that appears at the top of the results. Twitter adds a link below the Search box and you can run the search any time by just clicking that link.

Searching with the old Twitter interface

If your profile is still mired in the old Twitter interface, you can still search, of course, but getting things started takes a lot more work. Here are the steps to follow:

1. In any Twitter page, scroll to the bottom of the page.

In any Windows Web browser, press Ctrl+End to jump to the bottom of the page; in any Mac browser, press ⌘+End. In both cases, make sure the cursor isn't inside a text box (such as the What are you doing? text box).

2. **Click the Search link.** The Twitter Search page appears, as shown in figure 6.6.

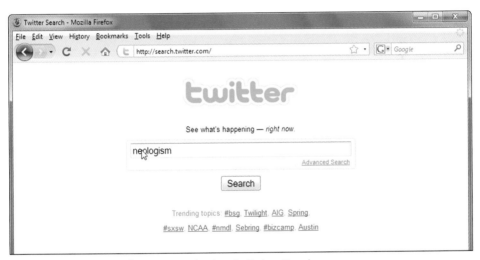

6.6 In the old Twitter interface, you search using the Twitter Search page.

3. **Type a search term in the text box.**

4. **Click the Search button.** You can also press Enter or Return. Twitter displays the tweets your search term found either in the text or the tweeter's username. Figure 6.7 shows an example results page.

6.7 The old Twitter search results show those tweets that match your search term either in the text or in the username.

note Not only do you use search differently in the old and new interfaces, but the search results themselves are different. Results (literally) are mixed as I write this, but the new search engine seems to be a bit more powerful than the old one, and often a search on the same term in both interfaces produces more results with the new engine.

Realtime search results

Whatever type of search you perform, you see the matching tweets under the heading Realtime results for *term*, where *term* is the search text you entered. The use of the word *realtime* (written, interestingly and a bit unusually, as a single word) means not only that you're seeing the most recently posted tweets that match your search term, but that Twitter is tracking your search term in the background while your results are displayed. If any new tweets are posted while you're checking out the results, Twitter adds a banner above the results:

```
x more results since you started searching. Refresh to see them
```

Here, *x* is the number of new results. You probably won't see this banner for obscure search terms, but if your search is related to some topic that currently has lots of Twitter buzz, the banner might appear surprisingly quickly. For example, I ran a search on "ncaa" when the NCAA Basketball Tournament was playing, and within a few seconds Twitter displayed the banner shown in figure 6.8 to tell me that three new matching tweets had been posted.

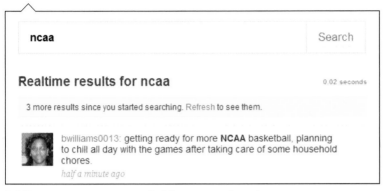

6.8 If any new tweets are posted while your search results are onscreen, Twitter displays a banner to let you know.

Twitter keeps updating the banner, too. In the few minutes it took me to write the last couple of paragraphs, the banner updated itself (see figure 6.9) to show me there were now 63 new tweets that matched my search!

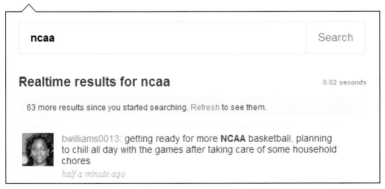

6.9 For popular topics, the number of new tweets that match your search term can grow alarmingly fast.

Fortunately, Twitter is smart enough not to mess with your displayed search results, so you can continue to study them without interruption. However, if you're curious to see the very latest results, click the Refresh link in the banner to rerun your search.

Performing Advanced Searches

A simple search on a word is often good enough to get a feel for what your fellow tweeters are saying about that topic, and you can often come across a few perfect posts that become immediate favorite candidates. (You can mark results as favorites in the new interface; see "Marking a search result as a favorite," later in this chapter.) However, if you want to really drill down into the depths of the Twitter database to unearth the true gems, then you need a more sophisticated approach. Here are some examples:

- Matching tweets that include a particular phrase or a particular collection of terms.
- Matching tweets that don't include a particular word or phrase.
- Searching for tweets posted by or replied to a person.
- Restricting your search to tweets posted within a particular date range.
- Searching for particular hashtags.

You can perform all these types of searches and many more by using Twitter's advanced search features. However, you once again come to an interface fork in the road.

The old Twitter interface includes an Advanced Search page that enables you to build fancy-schmancy search queries using familiar controls such as text boxes, lists, option buttons, and check boxes, as shown in figure 6.10. To get to this page, click the Advanced Search link in any search page.

As of this writing, the new Twitter interface does not include the Advanced Search page as an integrated feature. You do have a couple of choices, however:

- You can still navigate to the Advanced Search page manually by entering the address http://search.twitter.com/advanced into your Web browser. The downside to this is that your searches then use the old Twitter search engine, which as I mentioned earlier isn't as powerful as the new search engine. Also, there's no telling how long the Advanced Search page will remain a going concern once Twitter rolls out the new interface.

The new Twitter interface doesn't include the Advanced Search page in the test version that was available as I wrote this book. The new interface is a work in progress, and it seems more than a little odd that it currently excludes a simple front end for advanced searching. That may be remedied by the time you read this (fingers crossed!) thanks to a Murphy 's Law in technical writing: The day that a book is published is the day that the book's subject completely redesigns its interface.

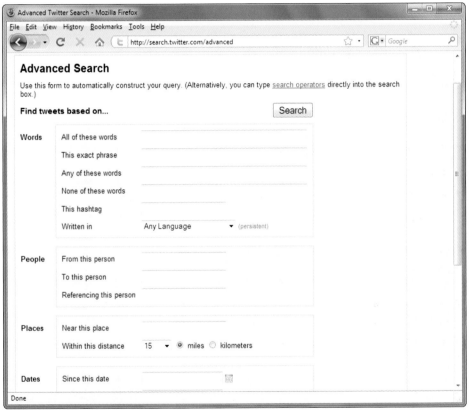

6.10 You can use the controls on the Advanced Search page to create sophisticated and powerful search queries.

- Almost all the options in the Advanced Search page have equivalent search operators, such as the word OR for the Any of These Words text box, and the words "since" and "until" for date-related searches. These operators work in the new search interface, so you can build your advanced queries and get the better results provided by the new search engine. The downside to this approach is that you need to mess with more complex operator syntax rather than the nice Advanced Search controls.

So in the sections that follow I'll show you how to build each query using the Advanced Search form and using the equivalent search operators.

Performing an advanced word search

A simple word search is to look for tweets that match a single word. Advanced word searches include matching a phrase, matching multiple words in any order, matching one word or another, and matching tweets that exclude a word.

Searching for tweets that include a phrase

If you want to search for a particular phrase, follow these steps to run the search using the Advanced Search form:

1. **In any search page, click the Advanced Search link.** The Advanced Search form appears.

2. **In the This Exact Phrase text box, type the phrase you want to match.**

3. **Click Search.** Twitter displays a list of tweets that contain the phrase.

However, this is one of those cases where no matter whether you're using the new interface or the old, it's easier and faster to not use the Advanced Search page. To search for tweets that match a phrase using the Search text box, enclose that phrase in quotation marks, as shown in figure 6.11.

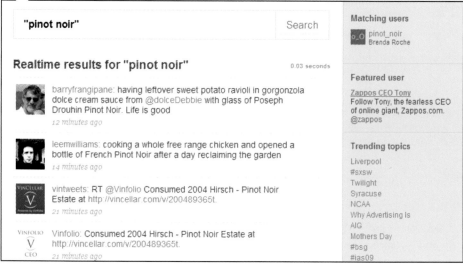

6.11 Place quotation marks around a phrase to match that phrase exactly within tweets or user names.

Searching for tweets that include multiple words

If you want to look for tweets (or users) that contain multiple words in any order using the Advanced Search form follow these steps:

1. **Click the Advanced Search link in any search page.** You see the Advanced Search page.

2. **In the All of These Words text box, type each word you want to match.**

3. **Click Search.** Twitter displays a list of tweets that contain all of the words you typed.

Once again, this is another case where it's just easier to use the regular Search box, no matter whether you're using the new interface or the old. Just type the words you want to match into the Search box in any order, as shown in figure 6.12.

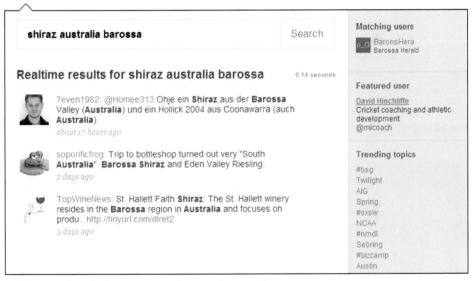

6.12 To match multiple terms, enter the terms in any order.

Searching for tweets that include one word or another

You can also search for those tweets that include one or more words from a list of words. Here's how you do this using the Advanced Search form:

1. **In any Twitter search page, click the Advanced Search link.** The Advanced Search page appears.

2. **In the Any of These Words text box, type the list of words from which you want Twitter to find its matches.** Remember that Twitter matches a tweet if it contains at least one of the words you enter.

3. **Click Search.** Twitter displays a list of tweets that contain one or more of the words you typed.

You can also perform the same search using the Search box directly. As a bonus, you also get to search for those tweets that include one or more phrases from a list of phrases. The operator to use is the word OR (which you must use with all uppercase letters), and you insert it between each word or phrase (with the latter enclosed in quotation marks). Figure 6.13 shows an example and the results it generated.

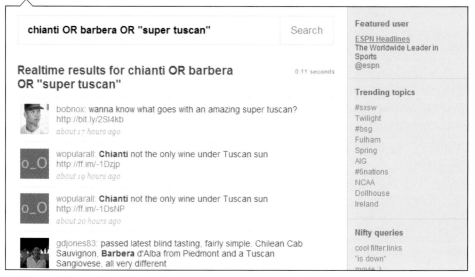

6.13 To match one or more items from a list of words and phrases, separate each item with the search operator OR.

Searching for tweets that exclude a word

It's often useful to search for tweets that don't include a particular word. For example, if you're interested in Chardonnay wine but you dislike the ones that come from Chile, you can tell Twitter to skip tweets that include the word "Chile." Here's how it's done using the Advanced Search page:

1. **In a Twitter search page, click Advanced Search.** The Advanced Search form loads.

2. **In the None of These Words text box, type one or more words that you want to use to exclude tweets.**

3. **Click Search.** Twitter displays a list of tweets that don't contain the words you typed.

You can run the same type of search using the Search box directly, but you can also search for those tweets that exclude the phrases you specify. The operator you use is the minus sign (-), and you insert it immediately in front of the word or phrase you want excluded from the matching tweets. (For a phrase, note that you must put the minus sign inside the quotation marks.) Figure 6.14 shows an example and its results.

6.14 To match those tweets that don't include a particular word, place a minus sign (-) in front of that word.

Running an advanced people search

Although most of your Twitter searching expeditions will scour tweet text for matching posts, it's also useful to search based on people. For example, you might want to see all the posts sent by a user, all the posts sent to a user, or all the posts that mention a particular user. You perform these people-related searches using either the Advanced Search for or the Search box.

Searching for tweets from a person

If you want to see all the tweets that someone has posted, it's easiest to navigate to that person's profile page on Twitter. However, what if you want to see only some subsets of those tweets? For example, you might want to see only those tweets from that person that include a certain word or phrase. For that, you need to take it up a notch and construct a search engine query.

Here's how you can search for tweets posted by someone using the Advanced Search page:

1. **Click the Advanced Search link in any Twitter search page.** The Advanced Search page appears.

2. **In the From this Person text box, type the Twitter username of the person whose tweets you want to search.**

3. **Use one or more of the text boxes in the Words section to specify which tweets you want to match.**

4. **Click Search.** Twitter displays a list of tweets from that person that match your other criteria.

You can also search for a person's tweets from the Search box. The operator you use is from:, and you insert it immediately in front of the username. In figure 6.15 I've constructed (and run) a search query that looks for posts from the user cshirky that contain the word media.

6.15 To return the tweets posted by a user, precede that person's username with from:.

Searching for replies to a person

Twitter replies are elusive creatures because you only see them on certain occasions:

- If the reply is sent to you.

- If the reply is sent by someone you follow to someone you follow.

Seeing a reply sent by someone you follow to someone you follow is the Twitter default setting, but you can configure your account to see every reply sent by someone you follow. See Chapter 4 to learn how to change this setting.

However, replies are public for most users, so it seems reasonable that there be some way to get at them. If you want to search the replies sent to a particular person, then you need to use the search engine, which also gives you the added benefit of being able to filter the result based on other search terms.

Here's how to search the replies sent to a person using the Advanced Search page:

1. **In a Twitter search page, click the Advanced Search link to display the Advanced Search form.**

2. **In the To this Person text box, type the Twitter username of the person whose received replies you want to search.**

3. **Use one or more of the text boxes in the Words section to specify which tweets you want to match.**

4. **Click Search.** Twitter displays a list of replies sent to that person that match your other criteria.

To search for the replies sent to a person from the Search box, use the to: operator, which you insert immediately in front of the username. In figure 6.16 I've built a search query that looks for replies to the user stevenbjohnson that contain the word *book*.

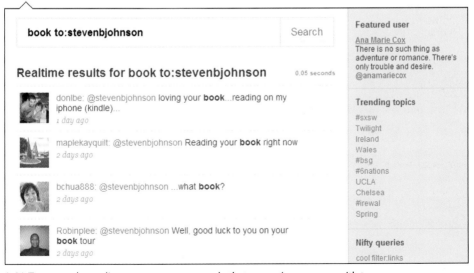

6.16 To return the replies sent to a user, precede that person's username with to:.

Searching for tweets that mention a person

Reply tweets always begin with *@username*, but plenty of tweets mention users by including @ *username* somewhere within the tweet text. It could be a retweet, a shout out to someone, an acknowledgment of an original post, a FollowFriday recommendation, or whatever. For these types of tweets, you can search for updates that include a reference to a user, possibly also filtered with other search criteria.

To search for tweets that mention a user with the Advanced Search page, follow these steps:

1. **Click the Advanced Search link in a Twitter search page.** The Advanced Search page appears.

2. **In the Referencing this Person text box, type the Twitter username of the person whose mentions you want to search.**

3. **Use one or more of the text boxes in the Words section to specify which tweets you want to match.**

4. **Click Search.** Twitter displays a list of tweets that mention the person and that match your other criteria.

To search for a user's mentions from the Search box, use the @ operator, which you insert immediately in front of the username. In figure 6.17 I've put together a search query that looks for mentions of the user wordspy that contain the text RT (so they're retweets).

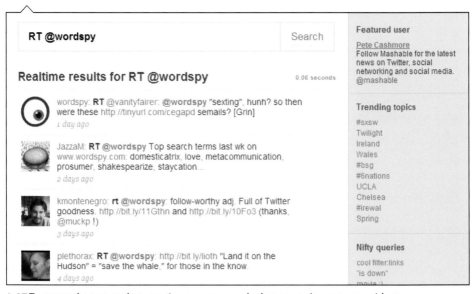

6.17 To return the tweets that mention a user, precede that person's username with @.

Filtering tweets by hashtag

You can tag a post with a particular topic by including in the tweet the topic word preceded by the hash symbol (#). For example, if you post a tweet related to Microsoft's Windows 7 operating system, you could include the hashtag #windows7 somewhere in the tweet. However, the real purpose behind hashtagging tweets is that they give you and other tweeters an easy way to search for a particular topic because the hashtag acts as a kind of natural filter.

Here's how to perform a hashtag search using the Advanced Search page:

1. **Click Advanced Search in any search page.** The Advanced Search form appears.

2. **In the This Hashtag text box, type the hashtag topic you want to find.** Don't add the hash (#) in front of the topic word; Twitter adds it for you automatically.

3. **Click Search.** You see a list of tweets that include the hashtag.

Hashtag searching is probably easiest from the Search box because all you have to do is place the hashtag operator (#) in front of the topic. For example, figure 6.18 shows a search for the hashtag #windows7 where the tweet also includes the sad emoticon :(.

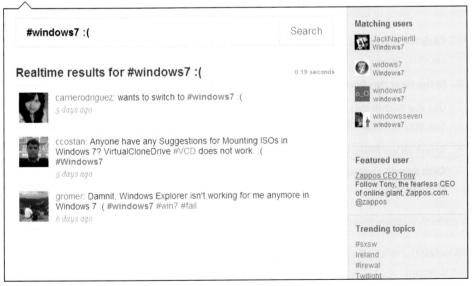

6.18 To locate the tweets that include a particular topic, precede the topic word with #.

For example, search Twitter for the word inauguration and you might get some tweets where people are still talking about U.S. President Barack Obama's inauguration, but you won't see the actual tweets sent that day because it's too old. You could click the Older link that appears at the bottom of each page of search results, but I assume you have a life outside of Twitter.

The problem is that Inauguration Day was January 20, 2009, and with Twitter sorting search results chronologically, the tweets from that day are simply too far back. To fix that, you can specify the tweets dates you want to see in the search results. You can specify a start date and an end date.

Follow these steps to search for tweets by date using the Advanced Search page:

1. **Click Advanced Search in any Twitter search page.** The Advanced Search form appears.

2. **In the Since this Date text box, type the start date.** Use the format yyyy-mm-dd. You can also click the calendar icon and choose the date from the calendar that pops up.

3. **In the Until this Date text box, type the end date.** Again, use the format yyyy-mm-dd, or click the calendar icon.

4. **Enter your other search criteria, as needed.**

5. **Click Search.** Twitter displays a list of tweets that were sent within the specified distance of the location.

To perform date-based searches using the handy Search box, you need to familiarize yourself with two operators:

- **since:** Use this operator followed by a date in the yyyy-mm-dd format to specify the start date.

- **until:** Use this operator followed by a date in the yyyy-mm-dd format to specify the end date.

You can use each operator on its own to restrict the search result on one end only, or you can use them together to set a date range.

To restrict the search results to a specific date, use the same date with both the since: operator and the until: operator.

In figure 6.20, I've cobbled together a search query that looks for tweets that mention St. Patrick's Day on March 17, 2009.

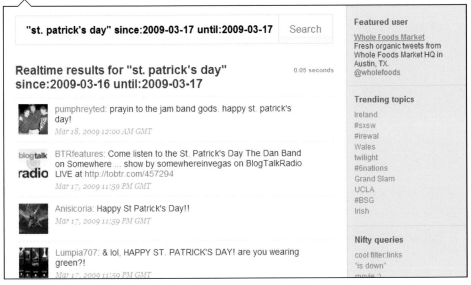

6.20 To return tweets based on the date they were sent, precede the start date with the since: operator, and precede the end date with the until: operator.

Locating tweets that contain links

For many Twitter fans, the most important tweets are the ones that contain links to other sites, because they're often the most interesting, the most useful, or the most fun. So it's great that the Twitter search engine includes an option that lets you specify that it should only return tweets that contain links.

Here's how to use this option from the Advanced Search page:

1. **Click the Advanced Search link in any Twitter search page to open the Advanced Search page.**

2. **Select the Containing Links check box.**

3. **Enter your other search criteria.**

4. **Click Search.** Twitter returns only those tweets that have at least one link.

To get your Search box-based searching to return only tweets with links, include filter:links as part of your search string. Figure 6.21 shows an example where I've search on the word cool and included filter:links to hopefully find some links to cool things.

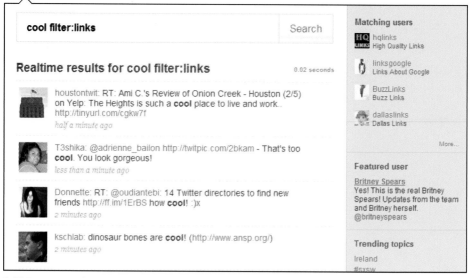

6.21 To return only tweets with links, add filter:links to your search query.

Adding Twitter Search to Your Web Browser

If you're using Internet Explorer 7 or 8, or Firefox (or indeed, any Web browser that supports OpenSearch; alas, Safari does not), you can configure the browser's Search box to include Twitter Search. Once you've done that, you can then type your search query in the browser and it passes it along to Twitter.

Adding Twitter Search to Internet Explorer

By default, Internet Explorer's Search box uses the Windows Live search engine. If you want to get Twitter in there, you need to create what's called a *custom search provider*. Here are the steps to follow:

1. **Navigate to the Twitter search page.**
2. **Run a search using TEST (all-caps) as the search string.**
3. **Copy the resulting URL from the Address bar.**

4. **Click the drop-down arrow to the right of the Search box, and then click Find More Providers.** Internet Explorer displays a list of search providers.

5. **Scroll to the bottom of the window and click the Create your own Search Provider link.** The Create your own Search Provider page appears.

6. **Click inside the URL text box and paste the address from step 3.**

7. **Use the Name text box to specify the name you want to appear in the Search box list (such as "Twitter").** Figure 6.22 shows an example that's ready to go.

6.22 Use the Create your own Search Provider page to create a custom search provider for Twitter.

8. **Click Install Search Provider.** The Add Search Provider dialog box appears.

9. **If you want Internet Explorer to use Twitter as the default search engine, select the Make this my default search provider check box.**

10. **Click Add.** Internet Explorer adds Twitter to the list of search engines.

To use Twitter within Internet Explorer, pull down the Search box list, and click Twitter (or whatever you name your custom search provider). Type a search query and press Enter and Internet Explorer displays the results in Twitter, as shown in figure 6.23.

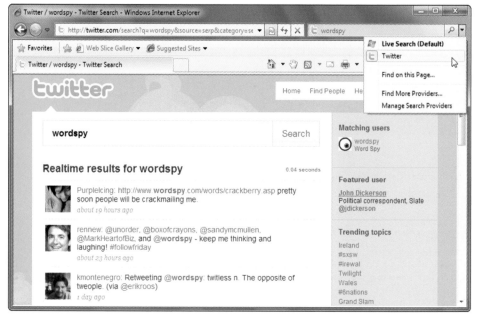

6.23 Internet Explorer customized to include Twitter in the Search box

Adding Twitter Search to Firefox

Adding Twitter Search to the Firebox Search box is quite a bit easier than with Internet Explorer. Here's all you have to do:

1. **Navigate to the Twitter search page.**
2. **Pull down the Search box menu, as shown in figure 6.24.**
3. **Click Add "Twitter Search."** Firefox adds Twitter Search to its list of search engines. Now that was easy!

6.24 To configure Firefox to use Twitter Search, choose the Add "Twitter Search" command on the Search box menu.

Working with Search Results

Once you've got your search results arrayed before you, it's just a matter of scrolling through the tweets, looking for the information you want, trying to find something that catches your eye, or just getting a feel for "What's happening now?" in that particular slice of the Twitter pie. There are three basic things you can do with individual search results:

- Check out the tweeter's profile page by clicking the username at the beginning of the tweet or by clicking the avatar to the left of the tweet.

- Click a tweet's link (if it has one) to visit the site.

- See the archive version of the tweet. In the new search interface, you do this by clicking the "about *time* ago" link under the tweet (where *time* is a time value such as "10 minutes" or "3 hours"); in the old interface, you do this by clicking the View Tweet link.

Besides these basic techniques, there are also a few other things you can do to work with the results you see. What you can do depends on whether you're using the old Twitter search feature or the new one:

- **Old Twitter search:** You can reply to a tweet (by clicking the Reply link); access a feed for the search results; send the search results as a tweet; and translate a tweet into another language. Also, if a tweet's link was shortened using TinyURL, you see an "expand" link beside the shortened address and clicking that link replaces the short address with the full version.

● **New Twitter search:** You can mark a tweet as a favorite and access a feed for the search results. Yup, that's it.

The next few sections cover these tasks, starting with the two measly things you can do with the results in the new interface.

It's possible, of course, that the only reason the new search interface has so few features is that the Twitter programmers just hadn't got around to adding them yet as I was writing this chapter. So by the time you read this there may be more tools for you to play with.

Marking a search result as a favorite

You'll often come across useful or fun tweets in your search results, but what happens when one day you stumble upon a perfect pearl of a tweet that not only scratches whatever itch caused you to perform the search in the first place, but that you know you'll refer to again and again? Why, save it to your Favorites list, of course! Here's how:

● **New Twitter search:** Hover your mouse over the search result to display the Favorite icon (see figure 6.25), and then click that icon. Twitter colors the icon orange to mark it as a favorite.

twitter from:mashable	Search

Realtime results for twitter from:mashable
0.04 seconds

 mashable: Reading: "**Twitter**, The Most Important Website Since Google?" http://tinyurl.com/cwxkj7
about 8 hours ago

 mashable: Happy Birthday **Twitter**! (PLEASE RT!)
http://bit.ly/cvtpS
about 17 hours ago

6.25 To mark a tweet as a favorite in the new search interface, click the tweet's Favorite icon.

- **Old Twitter search:** Click the New Tweet link to load the archive page for the tweet, move your mouse over the tweet text to display the Favorite icon, and then click the icon. Twitter marks the tweet as a favorite by coloring the icon orange.

Using a feed to monitor search results

Some searches are one-time-only deals where you run your search, check the results, and then return to whatever you were doing. Sometimes, however, you want to run the same search frequently. For example, you might want to know whenever a tweeter talks about a particular product or service, your company, or yourself. (Don't worry, everyone searches for themselves on Twitter; call it *egoTwittering*.) In those cases, it would sure be nice to have some way to monitor the search results.

I mentioned earlier that Twitter monitors your current search query in the background and kindly lets you know if new tweets that match your query show up. That's fine as long as you have the Twitter search page displayed, which these days isn't all that inconvenient because all the major Web browsers support tabbed browsing, so you can leave your search open in a tab while you move on with other things.

Of course, you'll eventually close that browser session or turn off or reboot your computer, so the next time you're back in the Twitterverse you'll have to run the same search all over again. To avoid that, a better monitoring idea is to create a feed for the search, which will let you monitor the search from the friendly confines of your favorite feed reader, such as Google Reader, NewsGator, or Bloglines.

If you're a TweetDeck user, you can also monitor a Twitter search within the TweetDeck window. See Chapter 8 for the full scoop.

Fortunately, creating that feed is just a click away because Twitter displays with each batch of search results a link to a feed for that search:

- **New Twitter search:** At the bottom of the sidebar, click the RSS feed for this query link.
- **Old Twitter search:** At the top of the sidebar, click the Feed for this query link.

Either way, when the feed page opens, copy the URL from the address bar. Now switch to your feed reader, create a new subscription, and then paste the address when the feed reader asks you for the feed URL.

Rather than opening the feed in your browser, right-click (or Ctrl+click on your Mac) Twitter's feed link on the results page, and then click Copy Shortcut (if you're using Internet Explorer), Copy Link Location (Firefox), or Copy Link (Safari).

Sending your search results as a tweet

When you're searching the Twitter landscape, you might come upon some sight or landmark that's particularly striking, so much so that you want to share your discovery with the people who follow you. That's very nice of you. How you go about doing that depends, yet again, on which search interface you've got.

Life is beer and skittles in the old Twitter search regime: near the top of the sidebar, click the Twitter these results link. This immediately posts a tweet that uses the following format:

```
Searched Twitter for query link
```

Here, *query* is the search string you used, and *link* is a handy link to the search results. Here's an example:

```
Searched Twitter for twitter from:mashable http://tinyurl.com/dy7359
```

Unfortunately, as of this writing, this convenience is nowhere to be found in the new Twitter search interface. To duplicate it, you need to follow these steps:

1. **Run the search.**
2. **Copy the resulting URL from the browser's address bar.**
3. **Click Home to return to your Twitter home page.**
4. **Type a short message that describes the search.** If you want to include the search query, click your browser's Back button, copy the search text, click your browser's Forward button, and then paste the string into the update box.
5. **Click Update.**

 If by including the full URL in your tweet you go over the 140-character limit, you need to shorten the URL. See Chapter 9 for some pointers to some URL-shortening services that are available.

Translating a search result to English

Twitter is a pleasingly global phenomenon, with tweeters tweeting from dozens of countries around the world. Chances are the people you follow write in English, but you never know what language might bubble up when you're searching, particularly in the new interface, which doesn't have a language setting.

In the old search interface, you can restrict the results by language. Click the Advanced Search link, and then use the Written In list to select a language.

In the old search pages, if you come upon results written in a foreign language, you have two choices:

- **Use the Show tweets written in list to choose English.** This removes any non-English tweets from the search results.

- **Click the Translate link.** Twitter uses Google Translator to translate the page. For example, figure 6.26 shows some search results written in French, and figure 6.27 shows the same page translated into English.

6.26 Some search results written in French

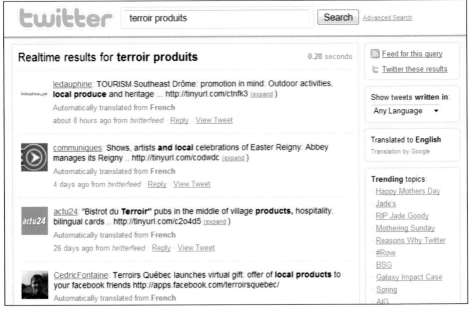

6.27 The same results translated into English

No joy here in the new search interface where the Translate link is noticeably absent. Is there a workaround? Of course! Here you go:

1. **Run the search.**

2. **Copy the resulting URL from the browser's address bar.**

3. **Navigate your browser to Google Translate at http://translate.google.com.**

4. **Paste the address into the Enter text or a Web page URL text box.**

5. **Under the text box, use the left list to choose the language you want translated.**

6. **Under the text box, use the right list to choose English (although this is the default value).** Figure 6.28 shows a Google Translate page ready to go.

7. **Click Translate.** Google redisplays the Twitter search results with the text translated.

6.28 If you have the new Twitter search interface, you can use Google Translate to translate any foreign language tweets that come your way.

Twitter Search Engines and Tools

Integrating search into the main interface shows the newfound importance of search to the Twitter powers that be. However, there's another sign that mining Twitter for tweet gold is becoming a big thing: the existence of a large and ever-increasing collection of Web sites that extend and enhance Twitter Search.

There's a kind of gold rush feel to all this as companies recognize a great opportunity: Twitter is going mainstream, for sure, and Twitter Search itself is merely okay, so there's a fantastic chance to become the de facto Twitter search engine. The result is a slew of Twitter-related search sites and tools. There are way too many to list here, so instead I'll just run through the ones I use most often, which are covered in no particular order.

As usual, the best place to keep track of the latest additions to the Twitter search collection is the Twitter Fan Wiki: http://twitter.pbwiki.com/Apps#SearchEngines.

Tweet Scan

When I'm in a simple mood (a not uncommon occurrence), I prefer to deal with sites that offer simple, uncluttered interfaces with nary a bell or whistle in view. For searching Twitter, the simple site I like is Tweet Scan (http://tweetscan.com/). As you can see in figure 6.29, Tweet Scan's home page includes just a humble text box for your search string (which supports the standard Twitter search operators), plus a tag cloud that shows the most popular Twitter topics. (The larger and more bold the type, the more popular the topic.) Search results are automatically refreshed every 90 seconds, you can reply to tweeters, post the results as a tweet, and there's an RSS feed address for each search.

TWEET**SCAN**

| | Search |

Search Cloud:

Rush Limbaugh #TCOT #frc #SXSW 3 mobile @guykawasaki HGTV Indeed Russell Simmons Sony adamcurry adware barilla battlestar british library cansecwest cloud computing comcast duke fastweb fiesta guarulhos hertz holiday indra jew leadership liebe los angeles maternity motrin nascar outsourcing owyang poland puma real estate recession scientology sharepoint spring sxsw SXSW bruce waiting weather

What is this? Sign in Find People Download API

6.29 Tweet Scan offers a straightforward interface for searching Twitter.

note For an even simpler Twitter search interface, check out Flaptor Twitter Search (http://twittersearch.flaptor.com/), which consists of just a text box and button.

Twitterfall

When I'm in a complex mood (rare!), I don't mind navigating sites that are festooned with options, settings, links, and other bric-a-brac. When it comes to third-party Twitter searching, perhaps the champion site for complexity is Twitterfall (http://twitterfall.com/), which shows real-time, constantly updated results for one or more search terms. The "fall" part of Twitterfall refers to the animation the site uses: as a new result appears, the existing results slide down the page.

When you access the Twitterfall site, it first displays the results for the currently popular Twitter trends. To run your own search, type a term in the text box in the Custom area, and then click Add. You're free to create multiple searches, and you can turn individual searches on and off using check boxes.

Figure 6.30 shows Twitterfall with two custom searches running: one for "iphone" and another for "ipod." Notice that when you hover your mouse over a tweet, the fall pauses and you see a collection of icons to the right of the tweet. If you're logged in to your Twitter account, you can use these icons to reply to the tweeter, send a direct message to the user (if you're mutual followers), retweet or favorite the update, follow the user, and view the tweet in Twitter.

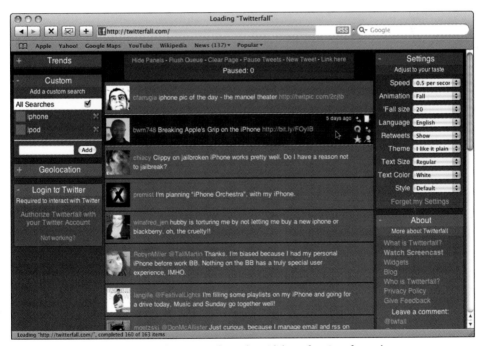

6.30 Twitterfall offers multiple real-time search results with lots of options for each tweet.

TweetGrid

If you want to monitor multiple search queries, you could set up each one as a feed in your feed reader, which is fine for results that don't change much. However, if you want to monitor these results in real time and you want Twitter interactivity such as sending replies and marking favorites, your feed reader would have no idea what you're talking about.

Instead, I highly recommend a great site called Tweet Grid (http://tweetgrid.com/). The "grid" part of the name means that you can display multiple Twitter searches, each of which appears in its own box, and those boxes are arranged in a grid. Several grid structures are available, such as 1×1 (a single search), 1×2 (two searches arranged in a single row with two columns), 2×3 (six searches arranged in two rows and three columns), and more. In each box you get a text box to enter your search string (you can use the standard Twitter search operators), and a Search! button to click to start the search. Figure 6.31 shows TweetGrid with a 2×3 grid running six different searches, all updating on-the-fly!

6.31 TweetGrid arranges multiple Twitter searches in a grid.

TweetGrid also lets you interact with Twitter. Type your username and password in the User and Pass text boxes, respectively, and TweetGrid uses that data whenever you want to exchange data with Twitter. For example, hover your mouse over a tweet and several icons appear in the lower-right corner of the tweet. (In figure 6.31, you see these icons in the first tweet of the top-left box in the grid.) These icons enable you to reply, retweet, or favorite the tweet, send a direct message to the tweeter (if you're mutual followers), view the tweet in the Twitter archive, and send the tweet via e-mail. You can also use TweetGrid to send a tweet.

 You can't save your TweetGrid layout, but you can add it as a bookmark in your Web browser. Right-click (or Ctrl+click on your Mac) the Full Address link, and then click Add to Favorites (if you're using Internet Explorer), Bookmark This Link (Firefox), or Add Link to Bookmarks (Safari).

Monitter

If your Twitter searching is all about location, location, location, you could add the near: and within: operators to your search queries. However, an easier way is to use Monitter (http://monitter.com/). This site lets you define multiple search queries, and the results of each query are displayed in a column. More importantly for location fans, you can filter all the results using distance and location, as shown in figure 6.32. For each tweet you get links to reply, retweet, or view the tweeter's profile, plus you see the tweeter's location.

6.32 Monitter lets you define multiple Twitter search queries and filter them by location and distance.

TweetBeep

Have you ever used Google Alerts, the service that sends you daily or weekly Google search results? It's an incredibly useful service, and if you've ever wished you could get the same convenience with Twitter, wish no more. With TweetBeep (http://tweetbeep.com/), you can define a Twitter search query, and then TweetBeep sends you a daily or even an hourly e-mail alert with the latest results.

After you create a TweetBeep account, you can immediately start creating alerts (although TweetBeep won't send you any alerts until you confirm your account by clicking the link in the e-mail message it sends you). Click My Alerts, and then click New Keyword Alert to display the New Keyword Alert page, as shown in figure 6.33. The layout of this page is nearly identical to Twitter's Advanced Search form. Fill in the fields to define your search criteria, click Save Alert, and then sit back and let TweetBeep do all the work.

 One of TweetBeep's sweetest features is the domain alert, which looks for domain names in tweet links, and it can even sniff out domains from shortened URLs. It's a great way to find out when a tweeter mentions your Web site. Click New Domain Alert, type your domain name, and then click Save Alert.

6.33 Use this page to define your Twitter search query, and then TweetBeep sends you hourly or daily results via e-mail.

Twemes

Hashtags are an easy way to track tweet topics, and you can use the hash (#) operator to search for a tag using Twitter Search. However, that only scratches the surface of the surface when it comes to hashtags. To delve deeper into this powerful tool, check out Twemes (http://twemes.com/), which specializes in viewing and searching hashtags. The Twemes (the name is a mashup of *Twitter* and *memes*) home page shows you a list of hashtags that have been recently updated, as well as a hashtag cloud (bigger and bolder means more popular).

 One quirk of the Twemes site is that it uses the word *tweme* instead of *hashtag*. Just remember that whenever the site talks about a "tweme," it's really talking about a hashtag.

You can also search for a hashtag by typing a topic (without the #) in the search box and clicking Search. In the search results, click Start live update to follow the hashtag in real time (see figure 6.34).

6.34 Using the Twemes site, you can search for a hashtag and then display real-time results.

AskTwitR

AskTwitR (http://asktwitr.com/) is a very basic Twitter search engine with one unique feature that makes it just a bit addictive: When you run a Twitter search from the simple home page, the first thing you see on the results page is a Google map. Within seconds, locations start popping up on the map, each of which is a tweet from the search results (see figure 6.35). Each pop-up shows the tweet text and the tweeter's avatar, and the pointer shows you the user's location on the map. It's oddly mesmerizing. Scroll down (if you can drag yourself away from the map) and you see matching Flickr photos, matching YouTube photos, and then (finally) the matching tweets.

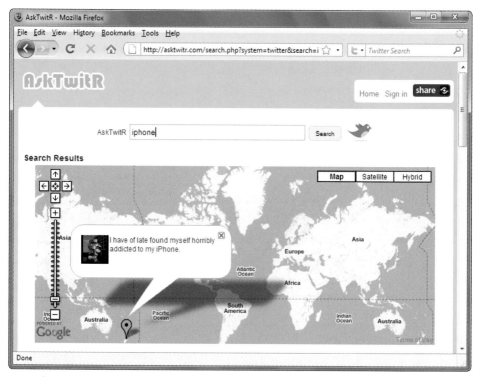

6.35 AskTwitR displays individual search results on a map so you can see where people are tweeting from.

BackTweets

If you want to see who has mentioned your Web site on Twitter, you could simply enter *domain. com* as a Twitter search (where *domain* is your domain name). However, the results miss all those links to your site that have been cut down to size with a URL-shortening service. (And because most addresses on Twitter are shortened, you'll miss a lot of tweets!) A better approach is to let BackTweets (http://backtweets.com/) handle this for you. You enter the address you want to search — it could be a simple domain name, a partial address, or a full URL— and click Search. BackTweets looks in the Twitter links for the address text you specified, and then displays the matching tweets. Best of all, it can even ferret out the address within a shortened URL (see figure 6.36), so you won't miss a mention.

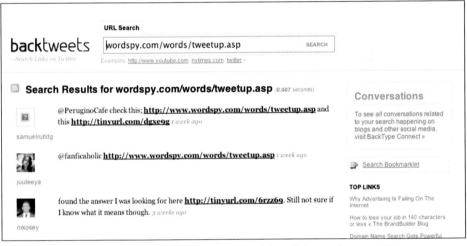

6.36 BackTweets can find addresses in tweet links, even if those links use shortened URLs.

TweetVolume

If you're researching a topic, it's often useful to run Google searches on different words and then compare the number of results that Google finds. If one term is vastly more popular than another, then you might decide to use the more popular term in a post or a marketing campaign.

For example, when I began writing this book, I couldn't decide how to refer to people who use Twitter: Twitterers? Tweeters? Tweeple? Tweople? For the most part, I use *tweeters*, if only because *Twitterers* is hard to say, and *tweeple* is a plural-only term.

However, what I should have done is use TweetVolume (http://tweetvolume.com/) to research each term within Twitter. TweetVolume is very simple: You enter up to five search terms, and the site returns the number of matching tweets, all displayed in a nice bar graph for easy comparison. Figure 6.37 shows the results for my four Twitter user terms (with Twitterati thrown in just for the heck of it). As you can see, tweeter is the winner!

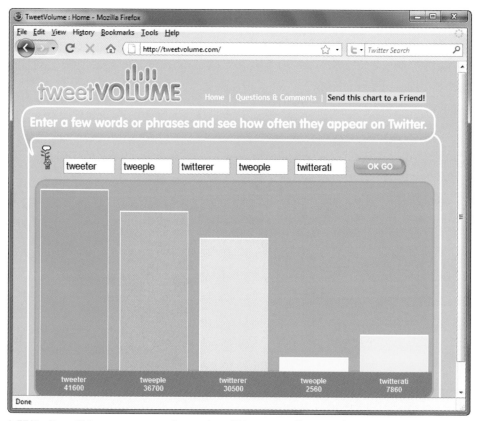

6.37 Use TweetVolume to compare the number of hits garnered by up to five search terms.

Where Can I Display My Twitter feed?

1 2 3 4 5 6 7 8 9

It's a rare Twitter user who doesn't want to have more followers. Few of us can aspire to the Olympian heights of the Twitterati and their hundreds of thousands of followers, but getting your count up to a few dozen or even a few hundred sure helps you get motivated to tweet. Good content drives up your followership, but how do you get people to see your content? In this chapter, you learn about two techniques that help: augmenting your regular Web site with links to your Twitter profile, and displaying your Twitter feed on your social networking site or Web site.

Adding Twitter Bling to Your Web Site

Now that you're well established on Twitter and you're tweeting away with your 140-character-or-less observations, ideas, and updates, it's time to fly your Twitter flag. If you have a blog, personal home page, or other Web site where you live your online life outside of Twitter, you should dress up that site with text or image links that take people to your Twitter home page. If people like what they see and use Twitter, they need only click your Follow button to get onboard; if they're not on Twitter yet, you might just inspire them to get an account so they can keep up with your tweets. Either way, you end up with more followers and life just keeps getting better.

Adding a Twitter link to your Web site

The simplest way to point someone to your tweets is to add a link to your Twitter home page. Ideally, you should place this link near the top of your page where people are sure to see it. Most sites have content that automatically appears on every page (such as a site header or a sidebar), and that's the ideal location because it means you only have to add the link once to that section and it appears automatically on all your other pages.

Creating a text link

If your Web host provides you with an online editor, use it to insert your links. How this works varies from host to host, but the following general steps are nearly the same with all hosts: Place the cursor where you want the link to appear and add some text (for example, "Follow Me on Twitter" or "See What I'm Doing on Twitter"). Select the text, click the editor's link tool, and then specify the address http://twitter.com/*yourname*, where *yourname* is your Twitter username.

If your site requires you to edit HTML to add a link, open the page or file in your HTML editor, place the cursor where you want the link to appear, and then type the link using the following HTML code (replace *yourname* with your Twitter username, and modify the link text to suit your style):

```
<a href="http://twitter.com/yourname">Follow me on Twitter!</a>
```

Creating a Twitter badge link

A humble text link is better than nothing, I suppose, but if it's Twitter bling you want on your site, then plain text just doesn't cut it. Instead, you need to get yourself a Twitter *badge* (also called a *button*), a small graphic that includes something Twitterish (such as a bird or some variation on the Twitter logo), which you then set up as a link to your Twitter home page.

Your first task is to locate a Twitter badge that you like. Here are some sites to check out:

- **Limeshot Design:** http://limeshot.com/2008/follow-me-on-twitter-badges

- **Randa Clay Design:** http://randaclay.com/freebies/free-twitter-graphics/

- **Shia Design:** http://siahdesign.com/archives/150

- **Vincent Abry:** www.vincentabry.com/31-logos-et-boutons-pour-twitter-2480

Figure 7.1 shows just a few of the excellent badges available on Vincent Abry's site (which is in French, but don't let that stop you).

Note that it's considered bad form to link directly to a badge on another site. Instead, you should download the badge you want to use to your computer, and then upload the file to your own Web site. Here are the instructions for using Internet Explorer, Firefox, and Safari to download an image to your computer:

- **Internet Explorer:** Right-click the image, click Save Picture As, choose a location, edit the file name, and then click Save.

- **Firefox:** Right-click the image, click Save Image As, choose a location, edit the file name, and then click Save.

- **Safari:** Right-click (or Ctrl+click) the image, click Save Image As, choose a folder on your Mac, change the file name, and then click Save.

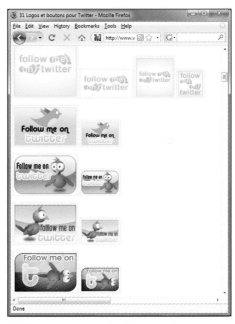

7.1 There are hundreds of Twitter badges available for free download, such as these from Vincent Abry's Web site.

Once the image file is safely stowed on your machine, upload it to your Web site using either an FTP program or the upload tool provided by your Web host.

If your Web host provides you with an online editor, use it to insert your badge. How you do this varies depending on the host, but the basic steps are pretty much universal: Open the page in the editor, place the cursor where you want the image to appear, click the editor's image tool, and then choose the Twitter badge file. Click the image to select it, click the editor's link tool, and then specify the address http://twitter.com/*yourname*, where *yourname* is your Twitter username.

If you add stuff to your site by editing HTML, open the page or file in your HTML editor, place the cursor where you want the badge to appear, and then insert the image and link using the following HTML code:

```
<a href="http://twitter.com/yourname">
<img src="filename" />
</a>
```

Here, you need to replace *yourname* with your Twitter username and *filename* with the name of the badge file (for example, twitter.png).

If you uploaded the badge to a folder, then you need to alter the code slightly. For example, if the badge resides in a folder named graphics, change the code to this:

```
<a href="http://twitter.com/yourname">
<img src="/graphics/filename" />
</a>
```

By default, images are aligned on the left side of the page (or whatever page element — such as a table — they're sitting in). If you want the image aligned on the right, add the following code: <img> tag: style="text-align: right".

Displaying a badge that shows your total followers

If you have a successful Twitter account that's amassed a sizable following, you might feel like bragging about it. I don't mean that you should cover the top of your page with a massive banner that shouts out your total followership. Please don't do that. I'm talking here about something a lot more subtle: a Twitter badge that not only points to your Twitter home page, but also includes a regularly updated count of your followers.

No matter how successful you are on Twitter, it's always considered bad form to brag (or even mention) how many followers you have. Other successful tweeters won't care, less successful tweeters might feel jealous, and I guarantee more than a few of your followers will abandon ship and stop following you.

The code wizards at TwitterCounter (whom you meet again in Chapter 9) offer just such a badge, and adding it to your Web site is a relatively straightforward matter of copying and pasting some code. First, use your Web browser to navigate to the following address, where *yourname* is your Twitter username:

```
http://twittercounter.com/pages/buttons/yourname
```

TwitterCounter displays a page that includes four button styles, as shown in figure 7.2.

7.2 TwitterCounter offers four styles of buttons, each of which links to your Twitter home and displays your total number of followers.

Below each button style you see a text box that includes some HTML code. Here's an example:

```
<script type="text/javascript" language="javascript"
src="http://twittercounter.com/embed/?username=wordspy">
</script>
```

This code points to a script that resides on the TwitterCounter site, and that script contains the necessary instructions for contacting Twitter and grabbing your current follower count. This all happens behind the scenes, and fortunately you don't have to give any of it a second thought (or even a first thought, for that matter).

After you decide which style you prefer, click inside the text box that appears below that style. Your browser automatically selects all the text, so press Ctrl+C (or ⌘+C on a Mac) to copy it. Now open your online or local HTML editor, place the cursor where you want the badge to appear, and then press Ctrl+V (or ⌘+V on your Mac) to paste the code. If you're working on a local copy of your page, be sure to upload the revised file to your Web site.

Adding a "Tweet This" link to your Web site

A great way to get the word out about your Web site or some content on your site is to get people to tweet about it. The problem is that it requires quite a few steps to construct a tweet about a site or page. Here are the general procedures:

1. Navigate to the page and copy the page address.

2. Switch to Twitter and paste the address in the update text box.

3. Return to the page and copy the page title.

4. Head back to Twitter and paste the title in the update text box.

5. Add your own text and then send the tweet.

Whew! However, you can do your would-be tweeters a favor by helping them to condense steps 1 to 4 into a single click of a link, which ought to make them more willing to tweet about your site.

I'm talking here about creating a "Tweet This" link (or perhaps "Tweet This Site" or "Tweet This Post" or whatever fits your situation), which you place strategically on your pages (for example, at the end of a blog post or article).

If you use an online editor provided by your Web host, place the cursor where you want the link to appear and add the link text (such as "Tweet This"). Select the text, click the editor's link tool, and then type the following general address:

```
http://twitter.com/home?status=Title (URL)"
```

Here, replace *Title* with the title of the page, post, article or whatever, and replace *URL* with the address of the item. Here's an example:

```
http://twitter.com/home?status=Word Spy (http://wordspy.com)"
```

If you need to edit HTML to add the link, open the page or file in your HTML editor, place the cursor where you want the link to appear, and then type the link using the following HTML code:

```
<a href="http://twitter.com/home?status=Title (URL)">
Tweet This
</a>
```

Again, replace *Title* with the item title, and replace *URL* with the item address. Here's an example:

```
<a href="http://twitter.com/home?status=Word Spy (http://wordspy.com)">
Tweet about Word Spy
</a>
```

Figure 7.3 shows how this code creates a Tweet about the Word Spy link on my site. If a tweeter clicks that link, the browser switches to Twitter, asks the user to sign in, if he isn't already, and then displays the specified text in the What are you doing? box, as shown in figure 7.4. Now all the tweeter has to do is add his or her own text and fire off the update.

7.3 A tweet invitation link on my Word Spy site

What are you doing?   111

Word Spy (http://wordspy.com)

Latest: Been working since 5AM. Wife's family coming over for
dinner tonight. Zzzzzzzzzz 1 day ago   update

7.4 Clicking the link in figure 7.3 loads the link's status text into the user's
What are you doing? text box.

 TwitThis (http://twitthis.com/) is a service that offers custom "Tweet This" links and
even includes a built-in URL shortener, which can save your potential tweeters
another step in the process.

Adding the Twitter Application to Your Facebook Profile

On the surface, Facebook, while ostensibly a member of the same social networking club as
Twitter, is a social horse of a different color. You can post photos and videos that people can
comment on; you can write on a friend's wall; you can join groups; and you're free to encrust your
profile with as many applications as you feel like configuring. However, although many Facebook
users take advantage of all these social knickknacks, the truth is that all most Facebookers do is
update their status every now and then.

As a nod to this reality, Facebook recently redesigned the user home page to display a "News
Feed" of posts from friends and, most tellingly, a "What's on your mind?" text box at the top that
you use to update your status, share information, or crack wise. Wait: a "What's on your mind?" text
box? Remind you of anything? Of course! It's Twitter, Facebook-style.

This leads to a very obvious question: If you're already using Twitter's "What are you doing?" box
to update your status, share information, or wisecrack, do you have to then repeat each tweet in
Facebook's "What's on your mind?" box? You could, I suppose, post different updates in Facebook,
but who has the time or energy to maintain two feeds? For that matter, who has the time or energy
to post the same updates on two different sites?

Fortunately, you don't have to. The kindly coders at Twitter have come up with a Twitter application
that you can add to your Facebook profile. This application includes an option to update your
Facebook status when you post to Twitter, thus killing two social network birds with a single tweet
stone (or something).

Caution

The only downside to posting tweets to your Facebook profile is that Facebook doesn't convert @usernames to links, so non-Twitterers might furrow their brows at these apparently nonsense references.

You can add the Twitter application directly via your Facebook account (click Applications, click Find More, and then run an application search for Twitter), or indirectly via Twitter. Here are the steps for the indirect method:

1. **Sign in to your Twitter account.**

2. **Direct your Web browser to http://twitter.com/badges.** The Get a Widget for Your Site page appears.

3. **Click the Facebook logo.**

4. **Click Continue.** The Twitter for Facebook page appears, as shown in figure 7.5.

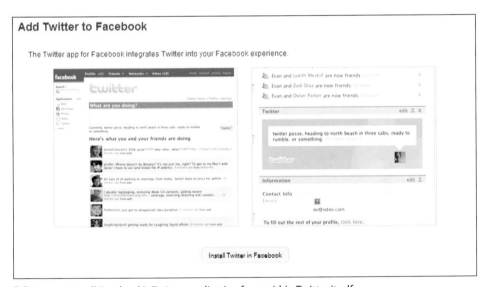

7.5 You can install Facebook's Twitter application from within Twitter itself.

5. **Click Install Twitter in Facebook.** If you're not already logged in to your Facebook account, Facebook prompts you to log in (or sign up, if you don't have an account). If you're already logged in to Facebook, the Allow Access page appears, so skip to step 7.

6. **Type your Facebook account's e-mail address and password, and then click Login.** Facebook's Allow Access page appears.

7. **Click Allow.** Facebook asks you to log in to your Twitter account.

8. **Type your Twitter username and password, and then click Log in.**

If you see an error message after you click Log in, don't fret about it. Just click your browser's Back button and all will be well.

You end up at the Twitter on Facebook page, shown in figure 7.6. (To get to this page in the future, click Applications, click Edit, and then click Twitter.) The Twitter application shows your friend timeline, as well as a What are you doing? text box, which you can use to post tweets from within Facebook. When you want to return to your real Twitter life, click one of the following tabs: Twitter Home, Profile, or Settings.

For easier access to the Twitter application, click the Bookmark Twitter link at the bottom of the page to add the Twitter application to your list of Facebook bookmarks. If you don't see that link, click Applications, click Edit, and then click the Edit Settings link beside the Twitter application. In the Edit Twitter Settings dialog box, display the Bookmark tab, select Bookmark Twitter, and then click OK.

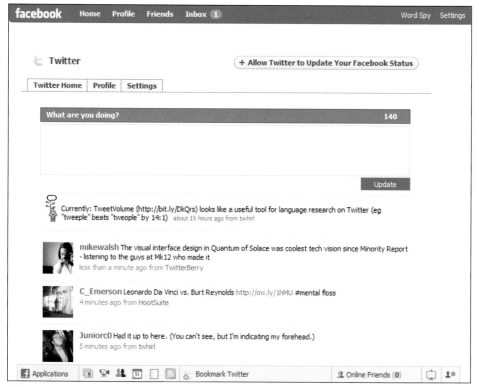

7.6 The Twitter application on Facebook

If you want your tweets to also get posted as your Facebook status updates, click the Allow Twitter to Update Your Facebook Status. When the Twitter application asks you to confirm, click Allow Status Updates.

 To turn off automatic status updates from Twitter, click Applications, click Edit, and then click the Edit Settings link beside the Twitter application. In the Edit Twitter Settings dialog box, display the Wall tab, select Never publish any stories from Twitter, and then click OK.

Inserting the Twitter Flash Widget on Your MySpace Page

If you have a MySpace account, you can let your MySpace friends know that you have a secret Twitter identity. Twitter offers a Flash-based widget that displays your recent Twitter updates. Actually, there are two widgets to choose from (see figure 7.7 a bit later in this chapter):

- **Interactive widget.** This widget shows your username, avatar, and the number of people who follow you. It contains a scrollable list of your last few tweets and also enables MySpacers to log in to their Twitter accounts and then interact with the widget by following you, replying to a tweet, or marking a tweet as a favorite. Tweet links also work, including @username links to Twitter profiles. This interaction is a great feature that will hopefully get lots of MySpace users to follow you.

- **Display-only widget.** This simple widget displays a shorter list of your recent tweets along with a link to your Twitter profile page. MySpace users can't interact with this widget, so it's less useful as a marketing tool for your Twitter account.

First, you need to get the widget code. Here are the steps to follow:

1. **Sign in to your Twitter account.**
2. **Navigate to http://twitter.com/badges.** You see the Get a Widget for Your Site page.
3. **Click the MySpace logo.**
4. **Click Continue.** The Which Flash Widget page appears, as shown in figure 7.7.

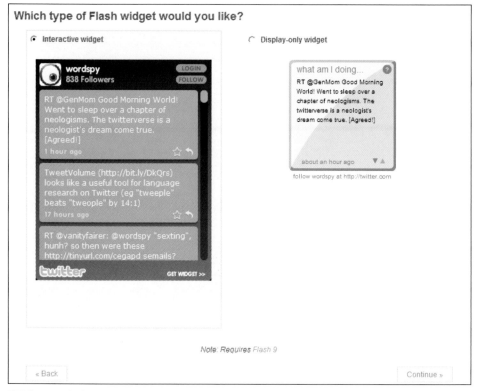

Which type of Flash widget would you like?

⦿ Interactive widget   ○ Display-only widget

Note: Requires Flash 9

« Back   Continue »

7.7 Choose which widget you want to grace your MySpace page.

 You need the Adobe Flash Player to see the widgets, so if Internet Explorer displays the Information bar telling you that the site wants to run the Adobe Flash Player Installer, click the Information bar and then click Install This Add-on, and then click Yes when asked to confirm. If Firefox tells you that additional plug-ins are required, click Install Missing Plugins.

5. **Select the widget you want to install, and then click Continue.** You see either the Set up your Twitter widget page (if you selected the interactive widget; see figure 7.8) or the Customize Your Widget page (if you selected the display-only widget).

6. **Customize your widget as follows:**

● **Interactive widget.** Use the Select a style list to choose a predefined design for the widget, and use the Widget size list to choose a width (narrow, wide, or full).

● **Display-only widget.** Click Badge Color and then click the color you prefer.

Set up your Twitter widget

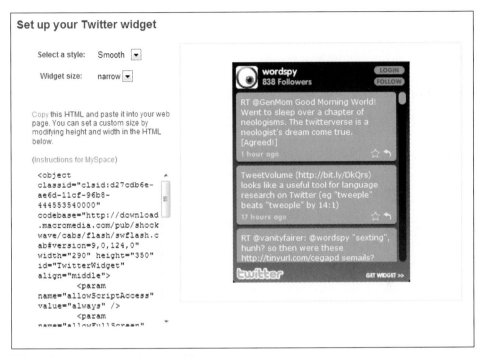

7.8 Use this page to customize your widget.

7. **Copy the code:**

    ● **Interactive widget.** Click the Copy link.

    ● **Display-only widget.** Click Copy to Clipboard.

With your code copied and ready for its MySpace debut, follow these steps to edit your MySpace profile:

1. **Log in to your MySpace account.**

2. **Click Edit Profile.** The Edit Profile page appears.

3. **Click inside the section where you want the widget to appear.** For example, you might want to use the About Me section or the General section.

4. **Press Ctrl+V (⌘+V on your Mac) to paste the code.** Figure 7.9 shows some code pasted into the About Me box.

5. **Click Save Changes.** MySpace displays a captcha for security.

6. **Type the letters you see in the image, and then click Save Changes.** MySpace adds the widget to your profile, as shown in figure 7.10.

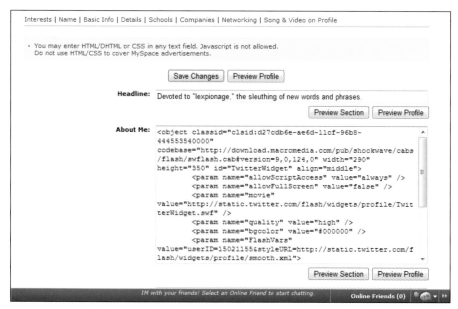

7.9 Paste the code into the section where you want the widget to appear on your MySpace page.

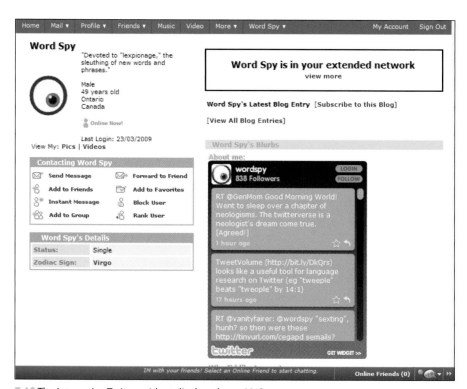

7.10 The interactive Twitter widget displayed on a MySpace page

Displaying Your Twitter Updates on Your Blogger Site

If you've got a Blogger.com blog on the side, you might want to spice it up by displaying your latest tweets. You can do that by adding a Twitter widget to your blog sidebar. This widget shows your most recent tweets (the default is 5, but you can easily customize that), as well as a follow me link to your Twitter profile. Tweet links (regular links and @username links) work, too, so your blog readers can check out the sites you include in your updates.

Here are the steps to follow to add a Twitter widget to your blog:

1. **Sign in to your Twitter account.**

2. **Point your Web browser at http://twitter.com/badges.** The Get a Widget for Your Site page appears.

3. **Click the Blogger logo.**

4. **Click Continue.** The Add Twitter to your Blogger blog page appears, as shown in figure 7.11. The right side of the window shows a preview of the widget.

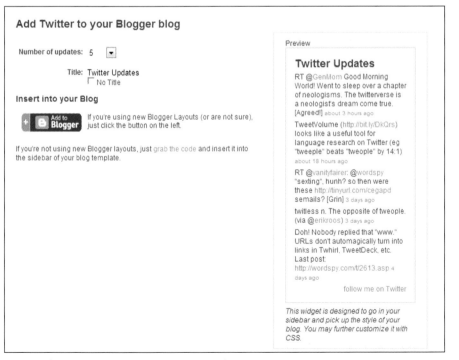

7.11 Use this page to customize your Twitter widget.

5. **Use the Number of updates list to select the size of the tweet list.**

6. **Use the Title text box to change the title if you don't like the default "Twitter Updates" title.** If you don't want a title at all, select the No Title check box.

7. **Click Add to Blogger.** If you're signed in to your Blogger account, the Add Page Element page appears, so skip to step 9; if you're not signed in, the Blogger: Sign In page appears.

8. **Type your Google account e-mail address and password, and then click Sign in.** The Add Page Element page appears.

9. **Use the Select a blog list to choose the blog you want to use, if you have more than one.**

10. **Once again you get a chance to edit the title by modifying the Title text.**

11. **If you want to adjust the widget code, click Edit Content to display the code, as shown in figure 7.12.** I talk about this code a bit later in this chapter and give you a few suggestions for customizing it.

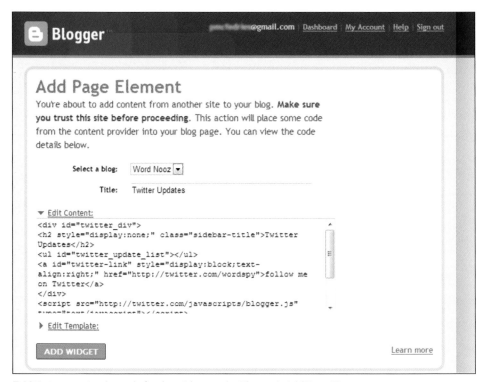

7.12 Twitter copies the code for the widget to the Blogger's Add Page Element page.

12. **Click Add Widget.** Blogger adds the Twitter widget to the Layout tab.

13. **Click Save.** Blogger saves the changes to your blog.

 Clicking Add to Blogger does *not* work in Internet Explorer 8 because it includes a security setting that prevents so-called cross-site scripting (XSS, for short). This is normally a good thing because malicious sites can use XSS to wreak all kinds of havoc. For now, you can disable this feature temporarily: Choose Tools⇨ Internet Options, click the Security tab, click Custom level, locate the Enable XSS filter setting, and then select Disable. After you're done, return to this setting and select Enable.

You can now click View Blog to see your blog with its shiny, new Twitter widget (figure 7.13 shows an example).

◘ Monday, March 23, 2009

Scientists Discover Elusive Soup-Nuts Continuum

COPENHAGEN—Researchers from Aalborg University announced today that they have finally discovered the long sought-after Soup-Nuts Continuum. Scientists around the world have been searching for this elusive item ever since Albert Einstein's mother-in-law proposed its existence in 1922.

"Today is an incredible day for the physics community and for humanity as a whole," said senior researcher Lars Grüntwerk. "Today, for the first time in history, we are on the verge of knowing everything from soup to, well, you know, nuts."

Lars Grüntwerk

Dr. Grüntwerk acknowledged that the search for the Continuum has been a grueling one: "We have had many missteps and false starts during the ten years that we have been working on this project. The number of different soups and nuts in this world and the number of possible permutations and combinations are both staggering and fattening."

"Our breakthrough came when my colleague Äärdväärk Sörenstäm and I discovered that we could represent both soup and nuts as abstract mathematical quantities," explained Grüntwerk. "After that, the equations became almost child's play and before long the entire Soup-Nuts Continuum was revealed in all its glory. We had a couple of Tuborgs to celebrate!"

 Twitter Updates

- RT @GenMom Good Morning World! Went to sleep over a chapter of neologisms. The twitterverse is a neologist's dream come true. [Agreed!] about 3 hours ago
- TweetVolume (http://bit.ly/OkQrg) looks like a useful tool for language research on Twitter (eg "tweeple" beats "tweople" by 14:1) about 19 hours ago
- RT @vanityfairer: @wordspy "sexting", hunh? so then were these http://tinyurl.com/cegapd semails? [Grin] 3 days ago
- twitless n. The opposite of tweople. (via @erikroos) 3 days ago
- Doh! Nobody replied that "www." URLs don't automagically turn into links in Twhirl, TweetDeck, etc. Last post: http://wordspy.com/t/2613.asp 4 days ago
- Top search terms last wk on www.wordspy.com: domesticatrix, love, metacommunication, prosumer, shakespearize, staycation, tanorexia, twitter 4 days ago
- sexting pp. Sending a salacious text message. www.wordspy.com/t/2613.asp 4 days ago

follow me on Twitter

7.13 A Blogger blog with a Twitter widget in the sidebar

Including Your Tweets on Your TypePad Blog

If you're a TypePad customer, you can let your blog visitors know about your Twitter shenanigans by adding a Twitter widget to your blog sidebar. Best of all, Twitter offers a widget that's not only configured for TypePad, but it will also add the widget for you automatically.

 The automatic insertion feature should work with most TypePad blogs, but the exception is if your blog uses TypePad's advanced templates, which Twitter can't update automatically. I'll show you how to do it by hand a bit later.

Adding the Twitter widget automatically

Here are the steps to follow to add a Twitter widget to your TypePad blog:

1. **Sign in to your Twitter account.**

2. **Send your Web browser to http://twitter.com/badges to open the Get a Widget for Your Site page.**

3. **Click the TypePad logo.**

4. **Click Continue.** The Add Twitter to your TypePad weblog page appears, as shown in figure 7.14, and you see a preview of the widget on the right side of the page.

5. **Use the Number of updates list to select the size of the tweet list.**

6. **Use the Title text box to change the title to something other than the default ("Twitter Updates").** If you'd prefer to go without a title, select the No Title check box.

7. **Click Install Widget on TypePad.** If you're signed in to your TypePad account, the Add a Sidebar Widget page appears, so skip to step 9; if you're not signed in, the TypePad login page appears.

8. **Type your TypePad account e-mail address (or username) and password, and then click Sign In.** The Add a Sidebar Widget page appears.

9. **In the Configure section, select the check box beside each blog where you want the widget to appear.**

Add Twitter to your TypePad weblog

Number of updates: 5 ▾

Title: Twitter Updates
☐ No Title

Insert into your Blog

[Install Widget on TypePad]

Note:This button won't work if your weblog utilizes Advanced Templates or Mixed Media Layouts. View the code to insert it yourself.

Preview

Twitter Updates

RT @GenMom Good Morning World! Went to sleep over a chapter of neologisms. The twitterverse is a neologist's dream come true. [Agreed!] about 3 hours ago

TweetVolume (http://bit.ly/DkQrs) looks like a useful tool for language research on Twitter (eg "tweeple" beats "tweople" by 14:1) about 19 hours ago

RT @vanityfairer: @wordspy "sexting", hunh? so then were these http://tinyurl.com/cegapd semails? [Grin] 3 days ago

twitless n. The opposite of tweople. (via @erikroos) 3 days ago

Doh! Nobody replied that "www." URLs don't automagically turn into links in Twhirl, TweetDeck, etc. Last post: http://wordspy.com /t/2613.asp 4 days ago

follow me on Twitter

This widget is designed to go in your sidebar and pick up the style of your blog. You may further customize it with CSS.

7.14 Use the Add Twitter to your TypePad weblog page to configure your Twitter widget.

10. Edit the title, if you feel like it.

11. Click Add Widget. TypePad prompts you to change where the widget appears in your sidebar. By default, the widget appears at the bottom of the sidebar, so you might want to move it higher.

12. If you want to configure where the widget appears, click Change Content Ordering, click and drag the Twitter widget to the new position, and then click Save Changes.

You can now click View weblog to see your blog with its brand-new Twitter widget (figure 7.15 shows an example).

NEWS OF THE WORD

Language news you won't find anywhere else (for good reason!)

UN Establishes Vowel Relief Fund

AIEA, Hawaii—Former United Nations Secretary General Boutros-Boutros Ghali and current United Nations Undersecretary for Alphabet Mobilization Yada-Yada Yada announced today the formation of the United Nations International Vowel Assistance Committee. UNIVAC's mandate is "to help the vowel-deprived wherever they may live and to fund vowel relief efforts in the hardest hit areas."

"We have a good stockpile of a's, e's, and o's," said Ng Ng, UNIVAC's Letter Distribution Officer. "We hope to have an adequate supply of i's and u's over the next six months. In the meantime, we can use our extra y's in a pinch."

"Vowels of every description are badly needed," said Cwm Pffft, an activist with the group Consonant Watch. "The people in places such as Srpska Crnja and Hwlffordd are suffering horribly."

When asked to comment on the news, writer and animated film voice specialist Sarah Vowell said, "I haven't the faintest idea what you're talking about. Leave me alone."

Posted on March 23, 2008 | Permalink | Comments (0)

Irate Grammarians Will See *You* in Court, Mister!

KALAMAZOO, Michigan—A group of disgruntled grammarians calling themselves "Mad, We Are, As Hell" has filed a number of civil lawsuits over the past few

TWITTER UPDATES

RT @GenMom Good Morning World! Went to sleep over a chapter of neologisms. The twitterverse is a neologist's dream come true. [Agreed!] about 4 hours ago

TweetVolume (http://bit.ly/DkQrs) looks like a useful tool for language research on Twitter (eg "tweeple" beats "twople" by 14:1) about 20 hours ago

RT @vanityfairer: @wordspy "sexting", hunh? so then were these http://tinyurl.com/cegapd semails? [Grin] 3 days ago

follow me on Twitter

RECENT POSTS

UN Establishes Vowel Relief Fund

7.15 A TypePad blog showing off a Twitter widget in the sidebar

Adding the Twitter widget by hand

If your TypePad blog uses an advanced template, Twitter won't be able to update your blog automatically. Not to worry, though, you can still do it by hand. Here's how:

1. **Sign in to your Twitter account.**

2. **Go to http://twitter.com/badges to open the Get a Widget for Your Site page.**

3. **Click the TypePad logo.**

4. **Click Continue to open the Add Twitter to your TypePad weblog page.**

5. **Use the Number of updates list to select the size of the tweet list.**

6. **Use the Title text box to change the title to something other than the default ("Twitter Updates").** If you prefer to go without a title, select the No Title check box.

7. **Click the View the code link.** Twitter displays the widget code in a text box.

8. **Highlight the code and press Ctrl+C (or ⌘+C on a Mac) to copy it.**

9. **Log in to your TypePad account.**

10. **Click the blog you want to use.**

11. **Click the Design tab.** TypePad displays a list of the advanced templates your blog uses.

12. **Click the Sidebar template.** The Edit Template: Sidebar page appears.

13. **Position the cursor where you want the widget to appear in the sidebar.**

Adding the widget to the top of the sidebar is the easiest option. Just position the cursor below the <!-- sidebar --> line that appears at the top of the template. For any other position, be careful not to insert the code within an existing module. For example, if you want the widget to appear after the Recent Posts module, position the cursor on the line below the </MTBlogIfArchives> line.

14. **Press Ctrl+V (or, on your Mac, ⌘+V) to paste the widget code.** Figure 7.16 shows the code pasted at the top of the sidebar template. For some ideas on customizing this code, see the section "Adding Twitter's HTML widget to your site" later in this chapter.

15. **Click Save.** TypePad saves the template and now shows your tweets to your blog visitors.

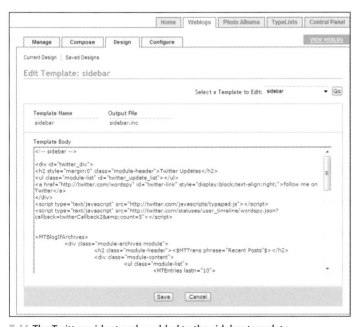

7.16 The Twitter widget codes added to the sidebar template

Adding a Twitter Widget to Your Site

If you don't have a Facebook or MySpace account, or a Blogger or TypePad blog, you can still give your site visitors the gift of your tweets. Twitter actually gives you a choice of not one, not two, but three widgets that you can add:

- **Interactive Flash widget.** This Flash-based widget shows your username, avatar, and the number of people who follow you. It contains a scrollable list of your last few tweets, and also enables visitors to log in to their Twitter accounts and then interact with the widget by following you, replying to a tweet, or marking a tweet as a favorite. Tweet links also work, including @username links to Twitter profiles.

- **Display-only Flash widget.** This simpler Flash-based widget displays a shorter list of your recent tweets along with a link to your Twitter profile page. Your site visitors can't interact with this widget.

- **HTML widget.** This HTML-based widget shows your most recent tweets (the default is 5, but you can customize that) as text, as well as a follow me link to your Twitter profile. Tweet links (regular links and @username links) work, so your site readers can surf to the sites you recommend in your updates.

There are quite a few widgets and plugins available for WordPress blogs. To see a complete list, check out the WordPress section of the Twitter Fan Wiki: http://twitter. pbwiki.com/WordPress. Also, there are lots of Twitter widgets available for any Web site. Go to Widgetbox (www.widgetbox.com) and search on "twitter" to see the available widgets.

Which widget should you choose? Personally, I love the interactive Flash widget because it's geared toward people with Twitter accounts, so I think it's more likely to help you gain followers. If you're worried about many of your site visitors not having the Flash player installed, then the HTML widget is the way to go.

According to Adobe, the makers of Flash, 99 percent of Internet-enabled desktops have Flash installed (source: www.adobe.com/products/player_census/flashplayer/). Seems awfully high to me, but you can at least be sure that most of your site visitors are likely to have the Flash player installed.

Adding Twitter's Flash widget to your site

To add one of the Flash widgets to your site, you first need to copy the widget code. Here's how it's done:

1. **Sign in to your Twitter account.**

2. **Surf to http://twitter.com/badges.** The Get a Widget for Your Site page appears.

3. **Click Other.**

4. **Click Continue.** The Which type of widget would you like? page appears.

5. **Select the Flash Widget option, and then click Continue.** The Which Flash Widget page appears.

> You need the Adobe Flash Player to see the widgets, so if Internet Explorer displays the Information bar telling you that the site wants to run the Adobe Flash Player Installer, click the Information bar, click Install This Add-on, and then click Yes when asked to confirm. If Firefox tells you that additional plug-ins are required, click Install Missing Plugins.

6. **Select the widget you want to install, and then click Continue.** You see either the Set up your Twitter widget page (if you selected the interactive widget) or the Customize Your Widget page (if you selected the display-only widget).

7. **Customize your widget as follows:**

- **Interactive widget.** Use the Select a style list to choose a predefined design for the widget, and use the Widget size list to choose a width (narrow, wide, or full).

- **Display-only widget.** Click Badge Color, and then click the color you prefer.

8. **Copy the code:**

- **Interactive widget.** Click the Copy link.

- **Display-only widget.** Click Copy to Clipboard.

If your Web host provides you with an online editor, use it to insert your widget code. How you do this varies depending on the host, but here are the generic steps: Open the page in the editor, place the cursor where you want the widget to appear, and then press Ctrl+V (or ⌘+V on your Mac).

If you edit your pages locally, open the page or file in your HTML editor, place the cursor where you want the widget to appear, and then press Ctrl+V (or ⌘+V on a Mac). Save your work, and then upload the revised file to your Web host.

Adding Twitter's HTML widget to your site

If you opted to add the HTML widget to your site, here are the steps to follow:

1. **Sign in to your Twitter account.**

2. **Surf to http://twitter.com/badges.** The Get a Widget for Your Site page appears.

3. **Click Other.**

4. **Click Continue.** The Which type of widget would you like? page appears.

5. **Select the HTML Widget option, and then click Continue.** The Customize and Get the Code page appears.

6. **Use the Number of updates list to select the size of the tweet list.**

7. **Use the Title text box to change the title if you don't like the default "Twitter Updates" title.** If you don't want a title at all, select the No Title check box.

8. **Highlight the code in the text box and then press Ctrl+C (or, on your Mac, ⌘+C) to copy it.**

If your Web host has an online editor, use it to insert your widget code. How you do this depends on the host, but here's the basic idea: Open the page in the editor, place the cursor where you want the widget to appear, and then press Ctrl+V (or ⌘+V on your Mac).

If you craft your site locally, open the page or file in your HTML editor, place the cursor where you want the widget to appear, and then press Ctrl+V (or ⌘+V on a Mac). Save your work and then upload the file to your Web host.

To ensure that your page still loads successfully even if Twitter is in Fail Whale mode (or having some other problem), cut the part of the widget code that starts with the first <script> tag and ends with the last </script> tag, and paste it near the bottom of your page (ideally, just above the </body> tag).

If you want to customize the Twitter widget code, there's not a lot you can do, but you're not without options. First, here's the default code (prettied up a little to make it easier to read):

```
<div id="twitter_div">
<h2 class="sidebar-title">Twitter Updates</h2>
<ul id="twitter_update_list"></ul>
<a href="http://twitter.com/wordspy"
   id="twitter-link"
   style="display:block;text-align:right;">
follow me on Twitter
</a>
</div>
<script type="text/javascript" src="http://twitter.com/javascripts/blogger.
   js"></script>
<script type="text/javascript" src="http://twitter.com/statuses/user_timeline/
   wordspy.json?callback=twitterCallback2&amp;count=5"></script>
</script>
```

Here are a few customization ideas to consider:

 To change the title, edit the text between the <h2> and </h2> tags on the following line:

```
<h2 class="sidebar-title">Twitter Updates</h2>
```

 To format the title, insert a style attribute in the <h2> tag and add one or more text formatting properties. For example, the following code displays the title with blue, 20-point text:

```
<h2 class="sidebar-title" style="color:blue; font-size: 20pt">Twitter Updates</
    h2>
```

 To change the text for the link to your Twitter profile, edit the following line:

```
follow me on Twitter
```

 To adjust the number of tweets displayed, edit the count value in the second <script> tag.

note To learn more about how to work with cascading style sheets, please see the Wiley book *Beginning CSS: Cascading Style Sheets for Web Design, 2nd Edition* by Richard York (ISBN 978047009670).

How Can I Take Twitter to the Next Level?

1 2 3 4 5 6 7 **8** 9

Twitter has the endearing trait of being sneakily addictive. Many people sign up assuming they'll just follow a few friends and maybe fire off the occasional update when the mood strikes. Before long, however, those few friends have turned into a few dozen, and tweeting withdrawal sets in whenever they haven't updated in an hour. If you find yourself with an unshakeable Twitter habit, this chapter certainly won't help! Here I take you through a collection of Twitter power tools that enable you to squeeze every last ounce of Twitter goodness from your account.

Twittering on the Desktop: Twitter Clients

I've mentioned elsewhere in the book that the real essence of Twitter, its secret sauce, if you will, is immediacy: a friend's update comes in, you read it; a thought surfaces, you tweet it; an interesting tweeter pops up, you follow her; a topic interests you, you search for it. If you happen to be hanging out on the Twitter site, then all of these Twitter itches (twitches!) can be scratched without delay (although constantly reloading your friend timeline to see if there's anything new gets old in a hurry).

The rub here, of course, is that few of us have the staggering amount of leisure time required to constantly monitor the comings and goings of tweets and tweeters on the Twitter site. We have memos to write, spreadsheets to build, empires (however small) to rule. We have, in short, day jobs that require us to focus on local tasks.

Fortunately, that doesn't mean you have to sacrifice the real-time Twitter experience. In fact, if anything it's an opportunity to enhance Twitter immediacy because you can install on your local PC a Twitter client application that constantly shows you the latest tweets from your friends, and enables you to send updates, replies, and direct messages, follow people, search Twitter, and more, all from the comfy and familiar confines of your trusty computer.

Unfortunately, Twitter desktop clients are thin on the ground. Or, I should say, good Twitter desktop clients are thin on the ground. There are quite a few programs out there, but most of them are fairly pathetic, and some of those even charge you for the privilege! To my mind, there are only two really good Twitter clients for desktop use — TweetDeck and twhirl — and I cover them in the next couple of sections.

Raising your Twitter game with TweetDeck

According to Twitter statistics site TwitStat (http://twitstat.com/), as I write this the most popular way that people interface with Twitter is via the Twitter site, although the percentage of users recently fell below 30 percent, and is dropping slowly but surely. That means that more than 70 percent of tweeters use some sort of client, and of those, by far the most popular is TweetDeck, with more than twice the number of users as the next most popular client.

That popularity isn't surprising because TweetDeck is loaded with features, and it wraps those features in an easy-to-use, attractive interface. TweetDeck isn't a Twitter client, per se, but more of a social media client because it can also integrate with other services, such as Facebook (currently being tested) and 12seconds. The focus here is on Twitter, of course, so I'll just take you through TweetDeck's Twitter-related features.

Getting started with TweetDeck

TweetDeck is an AIR (Adobe Integrated Runtime) application, which means it can run on multiple operating systems. As I write this, TweetDeck runs on Windows XP, Windows Vista, and Mac OS X, and there's a separate download for Linux. (Depending on when you read this, there may also be a Windows 7 version available.) Head for the TweetDeck site (www.tweetdeck.com), and click Install Now. Note that the installer first adds the AIR runtime files to your system and then it installs TweetDeck.

As I was writing this book, TweetDeck released a test version of the program that also integrates Facebook, which lets you send updates to Twitter, to Facebook, or to both services. It's a nice feature if you're a Twitterer and a Facebooker. By the time you read this, the Facebook feature could be integrated into the regular version of TweetDeck.

When you run the program for the first time, it prompts you for your Twitter username and password. When you sign in, the TweetDeck window appears, as shown in figure 8.1. As you can see, the TweetDeck window is divided into three columns:

- **All Friends.** This is your friend timeline, and TweetDeck checks for new tweets once a minute.

- **Replies.** This is your timeline of replies sent to you and retweets of your updates. TweetDeck updates this list every 12 minutes.

- **Direct Messages.** This is a list of the direct messages you've sent and received, and TweetDeck updates the list every six minutes.

TweetDeck is great and all, but it has one less-than-great feature: it plays a chirp every time you have at least one new tweet on your friend timeline. This gets supremely annoying after about five minutes, but you can save your sanity by turning it off. Click the Settings icon (it's the wrench near the upper-right corner of the window), click the General tab, and then deselect the Play notification sound check box.

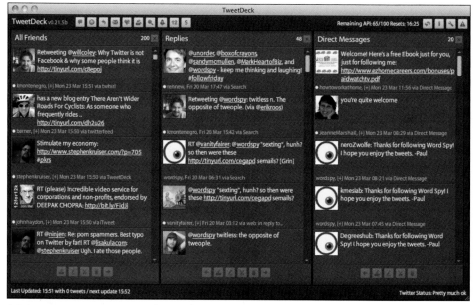

8.1 TweetDeck shows your friends' tweets, and your replies and directs, all in one place.

Working with tweets within TweetDeck is straightforward: move your mouse over the avatar of the tweet you want to mess with, and TweetDeck displays four icons:

- **Reply.** Click to send a reply to the tweeter.
- **Retweet.** Click to retweet the update to your followers.
- **Direct Message.** Click to send a direct message to the user (assuming the two of you follow each other).
- **Other Actions.** Click to see a menu that contains an impressively long list of commands, as shown in figure 8.2. Most of these commands are self-explanatory, but two are unique to TweetDeck:
  - **Add to Group.** This adds the user to one of your TweetDeck groups (described a bit later).
  - **Search.** This runs a Twitter search on the tweeter's username and displays the results in a new column.

When you're ready to post a tweet yourself, click the Tweet icon (the leftmost icon in the top toolbar). TweetDeck displays a What are you doing? text box, as shown in figure 8.3. However, this isn't your father's What are you doing? text box. Although there are buttons galore here, three are supremely useful to your average Twitterholic:

Shorten URL. Use this text box to type or paste a Web address that you want to include in your tweet. Make sure the What are you doing? cursor is where you want the address to appear, use the list to the right of the text box to select a URL shortening service, and then click Shorten. (See Chapter 9 to learn more about URL shortening.)

TwitPic. Use this button to share a picture with your followers using the TwitPic service (also described in Chapter 9). Click TwitPic, and then choose the picture you want to share. TweetDeck uploads the image to TwitPic and inserts a link to the image in the tweet.

TweetShrink. If your tweet text is running long, click this button (it's the downward pointing arrow to the right of the TwitPic button) to send the text to the TweetShrink service (once again, I cover this in Chapter 9). TweetShrink replaces certain words with short forms (such as ppl for *people* and twttr for *Twitter*) to reduce the overall character count.

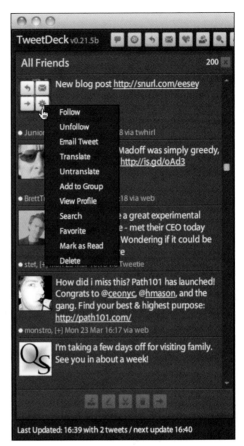

8.2 Hover the mouse over a user's avatar to see the tweet options, and click Other Actions to see a menu of commands.

8.3 TweetDeck's Tweet feature is loaded with useful options.

So much for the TweetDeck basics. The next few sections take you through four of TweetDeck's most powerful features: window configuration, tweet filtering, search monitoring, and friend grouping.

Configuring the TweetDeck window

One of TweetDeck's greatest strengths is its seemingly endless number of window confirmation options. You can add more columns, remove existing columns, move columns left or right, adjust the window size to show more or fewer columns, and even shrink the window down to a single column. Here are the basic techniques to use:

- **Adding a column.** With the exception of the Tweet button, you click the buttons along the top of the TweetDeck window (the ones to the left, that is) to control the columns you see in the TweetDeck window. Besides the All Friends, Replies, and Direct Messages columns, which are displayed by default, you have a half dozen other options: Favorites, Group (see the section "Creating a TweetDeck group"), Twitter Search (see the section "Monitoring a search"), TwitScoop (displays hot Twitter topics as determined by the TwitScoop service; see Chapter 9), and two services that require accounts — 12seconds and StockTwits.

- **Removing a column.** If you don't use a particular column, you should remove it to reduce clutter in the TweetDeck window. Click the X in the upper-right corner of the column, and then click the Yes icon when TweetDeck asks you to confirm.

> When you click X to remove a column, TweetDeck asks you to confirm, and the dialog box includes an apparently ominous warning: "This action cannot be undone - choose wisely". This warning is patently wrong for the All Friends, Replies, Direct Messages, and Favorites columns, because you need only click the corresponding toolbar button to add these columns back into the window.

- **Changing a column's position.** You can move a column's position within the TweetDeck window by clicking the left and right arrow buttons that appear in the toolbar below each column. For example, if you have more columns than can fit within the TweetDeck window, a horizontal scroll bar appears so you can scroll your columns. If you find yourself constantly scrolling to a column you use frequently, consider moving the column to the left so that it's back onscreen.

- **Using Single column view.** If you have a second monitor, a great idea is to display the TweetDeck on that monitor so you can keep an eye on your columns. If you're stuck with a single monitor, one alternative is to shrink the TweetDeck window down to a single column, and then move the window to the side of your monitor so that it's out of the way of your regular work. To make this happen, click the Single column view icon (it's third from the right in the upper-right corner of the window).

If you end up with more columns than can fit on your screen, you can configure TweetDeck to display narrower columns, which might improve things. Click the Settings icon (the wrench in the upper-right corner), select the Narrow columns check box in the General tab, and then click Save.

Filtering tweets

If you follow tons of people, then you're no doubt well aware that the tweets come in fast and furious, and keeping up is a full-time job that threatens to undermine your real full-time job. TweetDeck can help here by letting you filter a timeline to remove tweets that match some criteria, or to only shows tweets that match some criteria. Your criteria can be one or more of the following:

- **Tweet text.** You specify a word or phrase and TweetDeck looks for matches within the text of each update.

- **Username.** You specify a word and TweetDeck looks for matches within the tweeter usernames.

- **Source.** You specify a word and TweetDeck looks for matches within the source of each tweet.

- **Timeframe.** You specify a number and TweetDeck matches tweets that were posted within that number of hours.

The source refers to the client that the tweeter used to post the update. For example, updates sent via the Twitter site have the source web; not surprisingly, if a tweet was posted through TweetDeck, the source text is TweetDeck.

Here are the steps to follow to filter a column:

1. **Click the Filter the tweets in this column button.** This is the second button from the left in the column's toolbar (unless you're working with the leftmost column, in which case it's the leftmost button). TweetDeck displays the filter controls.

2. **Use the left list to choose the filter property you want to use: Tweet Text, User Name, Source, or TimeFrame.**

3. **Use the second list to choose either Include (+) or Exclude (-).** If you choose Include, TweetDeck only displays those tweets that match your criteria; if you choose Exclude, TweetDeck does not display those tweets that match your criteria.

4. **Use the box to type your criteria text (or number, if you're creating a TimeFrame filter).** If you enter multiple words, TweetDeck treats them as a phrase. TweetDeck filters the column, as shown in figure 8.4, where I'm filtering my All Friends column to show only the posts that include twitter in the text.

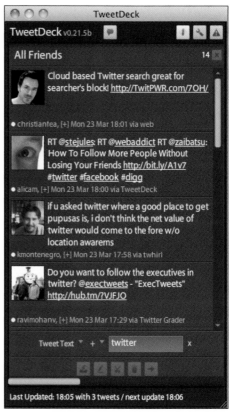

8.4 Use a filter to cut a long list of tweets down to a manageable size.

Monitoring a search

You saw in Chapter 6 that Twitter's search feature is a great way to get a feel for what Twitterers are currently saying about some topic. If you have a long term interest in that topic, then you probably want to monitor the search results over time. Rather than rerunning the search periodically, I told you in Chapter 6 about a few services that can do the monitoring for you.

However, why bother with yet another Twitter tool when you can get the same result using TweetDeck? With TweetDeck you can create a column of tweets based on a Twitter search, and TweetDeck will constantly monitor that search and display the results in the column. Even better, you can create multiple search columns if you need to track multiple search queries. Nice!

Here are the steps required to create a search column in TweetDeck:

1. **Click the Twitter Search button in the toolbar.** It's the one with the magnifying glass icon. TweetDeck prompts you for your search string, as shown in figure 8.5.

8.5 Type a Twitter search string to define your TweetDeck search column.

2. **Use the text box to type your search query.** The dialog box mentions that you can use AND, OR, and quotations marks, but actually any official Twitter search operator works here (see Chapter 6 for the details).

3. **Press Enter or Return.** TweetDeck creates the new column and displays the search results, as shown in figure 8.6. Note that you'll need to scroll the TweetDeck window to the right to see the new column.

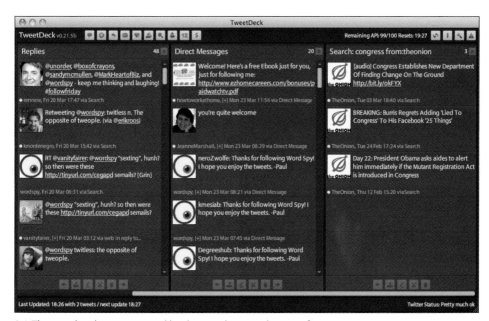

8.6 The search column generated by the search query shown in figure 8.5.

Creating a TweetDeck group

If you have lots of Twitter pals, your All Friends column on TweetDeck can often get quite noisy. That cocktail party-like hubbub is part of the Twitter appeal, but there may be times when you'd prefer something more like a quiet night out with a few friends. For example, if you and a few of your friends are working on a project, tweets from those friends will probably be more important to you than the other tweets that come your way. Similarly, if you're at work you might prefer to concentrate on just what your co-workers have to say.

This kind of thing just isn't possible with the Twitter Web site, but TweetDeck offers a Group feature that lets you gather a subset of your friends into a group, and TweetDeck then displays just the tweets from those people in a separate column. This is a perfect solution because you can still keep an eye on the raucous goings-on in your All Friends column, but the tweets you really want to see are conveniently laid out for you in your new Group column. Even better, TweetDeck lets you define multiple groups, so you can keep track of all your different factions.

Here's how it works:

1. **Click the Group button in the toolbar.** It's the icon that shows a couple of people. TweetDeck displays the Add a New Group column.

2. **Type a name for the group.**

3. **Select the check box beside each user you want to include in the group, as shown in figure 8.7.**

8.7 Type a group name and then select the check box beside each person you want in your group.

4. **Click Save Group.** TweetDeck creates the new column and displays the tweets from just the group members, as shown in figure 8.8.

8.8 A TweetDeck group shows the tweets from just the members of the group.

Controlling Twitter with twhirl

After TweetDeck, the next most popular Twitter desktop client (at least as I write this) is twhirl, and this popularity is well-founded. twhirl is a solid Twitter client that performs all the basic tweeting chores with ease, throws in a couple of extra goodies to sweeten the pot, and offers one thing that even the mighty TweetDeck can't do: It can handle multiple Twitter accounts.

Giving twhirl a whirl

twhirl is an AIR (Adobe Integrated Runtime) application, so it runs on multiple operating systems, including (as I write) Windows 2000, Windows XP, Windows Vista, and Mac OS X. (I expect you'll see support for Windows 7 added soon after Microsoft's latest operating system ships.) Point your favorite Web browser at the twhirl site (www.twhirl.org), and click Install Now. The installation program first installs the AIR runtime files (if your computer doesn't already have them), and then it installs twhirl.

Setting up your Twitter accounts

When you first launch twhirl, you see the Accounts tab, which is where you manage your Twitter accounts. Here's how to get started:

1. **Make sure the pop-up list shows Twitter.** twhirl also supports identi.ca, laconi.ca, Friendfeed, and Seesmic, but I'll just stick to Twitter business here.

2. **Type your Twitter username in the text box, and then click the plus sign (+).** twhirl adds the username to the Accounts list.

3. **Repeat step 2 for each of your Twitter accounts.** Figure 8.9 shows the Accounts tab with a couple of Twitter accounts added.

4. **Click the Twitter account you want to use.**

5. **Click Connect.** twhirl prompts you for your Twitter account password.

6. **Type your password, and then click Login.**

7. **Repeat steps 4 through 6 to log in to other Twitter accounts.** twhirl displays each account in a separate window.

Figure 8.10 shows a typical twhirl window. The default view shows your friends timeline in the bulk of the window, and an update text box, which twhirl calls the input panel, at the bottom.

To return to the Accounts tab after you've closed it, click the Configuration button (it's the wrench icon near the upper-right corner of the window), and then click Open Accounts.

8.9 You can use twhirl to manage multiple Twitter accounts.

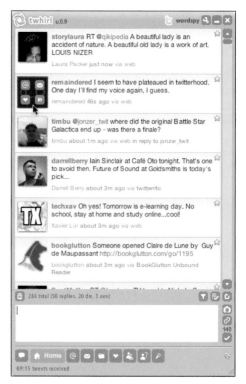

8.10 When you first open a Twitter account in twhirl, you see a timeline of your friends' tweets.

Working with tweets

To work with a tweet, move your mouse over the avatar of the person who sent the tweet. As shown in figure 8.10 (see the second tweet from the top), twhirl displays four icons:

- **Send reply.** Click to send a reply to the tweeter.

- **Send direct message.** Click to send a direct message to the user (as long as you follow each other, of course).

- **Favor.** Click to mark the tweet as a favorite.

- **Retweet.** Click to retweet the message to your followership.

When new tweets come in, twhirl beeps the speaker and displays a pop-up window briefly. If you've got a couple of account windows open and you've got a lot of incoming tweets, the incessant beeping and notifying is enough to drive even the most level-headed among us around the bend. To fix this, click the Configuration button (the wrench icon), click the Notify tab, and then deselect the Play sound check box and the Show notification windows check box.

If you want to gain a bit of control over a lengthy list of tweets, click Toggle filter (it's the funnel icon), and then use the Filter text box to specify a filter:

- To show only those tweets that include a particular word, type that word and press Enter or Return.

- To hide those tweets that include a particular word, type a minus sign (-), type the word, and then press Enter or Return.

Posting a tweet

As far as shipping out your own tweets goes, click inside the input panel and start typing at will. twhirl has two extra doohickeys that you might find useful when constructing a tweet:

- **Shorten URL.** Click this icon (it looks like a two-link chain) to open the dialog box shown in figure 8.11. Type (or paste) the address in the URL text box, select a site from the Service pop-up (some sites require a login, so fill in your credentials if needed), and then click Shorten. (See Chapter 9 for more about URL shortening.)

8.11 Click the Shorten URL icon to make a long Web address Twitter-friendly.

Share an image. Click this icon (it looks like a camera) to share a photo with your followers using the TwitPic service (also described in Chapter 9). Choose the picture you want to share, and then click Post image. twhirl uploads the image to TwitPic and inserts a link to the image in the tweet.

Navigating twhirl

twhirl's interface is a simple one-thing-at-a-time affair that lets you focus on one aspect of your Twitter life. The friend timeline from your Twitter home page is the default view — twhirl calls this a panel, but twhirl actually has eight panels in total, and you navigate among them by clicking the icons at the bottom of the window. Here's a summary:

Toggle input panel. Click this (it's the speech bubble icon) to hide or show the input panel. (This applies to all the views, so this option isn't a separate view per se.)

Home. Click this to see your friend timeline.

Replies. Click this (it's the @ icon) to see the replies sent to you.

Directs. Click this (it's the envelope icon) to see the direct messages sent to you.

Archive. Click this (it's the folder icon) to see the tweets you've sent.

Favorites. Click this (it's the heart icon) to see the tweets you've marked as faves.

Friends/Followers. Click this (it's the people icon) to see two lists: one for your friends and one for your followers.

Lookup. Click this (it's the person with a question mark icon) to look up a tweeter's profile. In the text box that appears, type the username and then press Enter or Return. twhirl displays the user's profile data and his or her recent tweets, as shown in figure 8.12.

Search. Click this (it's the magnifying glass icon) to run a Twitter search. Use the text box to type your search query, including any of the standard Twitter search operators.

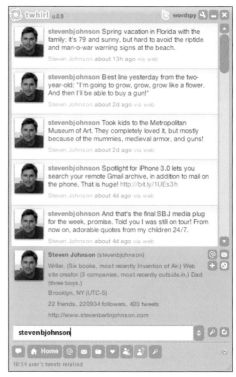

8.12 Click Lookup and type a username to see that person's profile and recent tweets.

The keyboard shortcuts in Table 8.1 don't work in Lookup and Search panels because when you choose one of those panels you end up in a text box.

twhirl also offers some useful keyboard shortcuts for navigating the window, which I've summarized in Table 8.1.

Table 8.1 Keyboard Shortcuts for Navigating twhirl

Press	To
Ctrl+Left arrow	Move to next panel to the left
Ctrl+Right arrow	Move to next panel to the right
T or F1	Display the Home panel
R or F2	Display the Replies panel
A or F3	Display the Archive panel
D or F4	Display the Directs panel
S or F5	Display the Favorites panel
F or F6	Display the Friends/Followers panel
L or F7	Display the Lookup panel
Y or F8	Display the Search panel
U or F12	Display the input panel and move the cursor inside the panel
M	Open the Accounts window
O	Open the configuration window

twhirl has a setting that lets you keep it on top of all your other windows, which is great for keeping an eye on your tweets. Even better, you can configure twhirl to fade when it's not active, so you can see the window you're working in. Click the Configuration button (the wrench icon), click the General tab, and select the Always on top check box. Click the Visual tab, and then adjust the Opacity value to taste (the lower the value, the more twhirl fades when it's not active).

Twittering on the Web: Twitter Web Sites

In the Anything You Can Do I Can Do Better Department, a number of Web sites have sprung up out of the ether in recent times to handle your tweeting chores, and their aim is to out-Twitter Twitter. They do that by offering useful features that tweeters crave, such as URL shortening, image sharing, and real-time updates. Toss in the advantage that you can use these sites to manipulate your Twitter world from any remote location where you have Web access, and Web site-based tweeting becomes a viable alternative to the desktop variety.

iTweet

iTweet (http://itweet.net/) is a full-featured Twitter interface with enough e-bells and e-whistles to keep most Twitterers tweeting contentedly. After you log on with your Twitter username and password, you see the main iTweet interface, as shown in figure 8.13. The page is divided into two vertical sections:

⊚ The left column includes a posting area at the top, and your friends' tweets below. The timeline is updated automatically (a feature that iTweet calls Autorefresh), so right off the bat iTweet is a step ahead of the Twitter site.

8.13 Click Lookup, and then type a username to see that person's profile and recent tweets.

- The right column shows your profile info, your most recent tweet, and boxes for searching Twitter, configuring iTweet settings, and learning iTweet.

You work with the tweets by using the icons that appear on the right side of each update:

- **Retweet.** Click the RT icon to retweet the message to your followers.
- **Favorite.** Click the star icon to mark the tweet as a favorite.
- **Reply.** Click the @ icon to send a reply to the tweeter.
- **In reply to.** If the update is a reply, click this text to see the original tweet that the update is in reply to. This is a really nice feature, and it's often indispensable in letting you figure out what the heck someone's talking about.

To see a tweeter's profile data, click the person's avatar. To switch the display to a user's tweets, click the person's username (click Home at the top of the page to return to your regularly scheduled timeline).

When you get the urge to share, click inside the text box at the top of the page and type your missive. iTweet has three tweeting tools that you'll want to get to know:

- **URL shortener.** Click this tool, type a Web address in the Enter a URL to shorten text box, and then click Shorten. (See Chapter 9 for more about URL shortening.)
- **TwitPic.** Click this tool to share a photo with your followers using the TwitPic service (also described in Chapter 9). Type a description in the text box that appears, click Upload, and then choose the picture you want to share. iTweet uploads the image to TwitPic and posts the tweet.
- **Symbols.** Click this tool to display a collection of characters (see figure 8.14). If you see a symbol that would go well with your tweet text, copy the symbol and paste into your tweet.

If you want your tweet to be a direct message, click the Send direct button, type the username in the Direct Message to text box, and then click Send DM.

To check out iTweet's other sections, click the links at the top of the page:

- **Home.** Click to see your friend timeline.
- **Replies.** Click to see the replies sent to you.
- **Direct.** Click to see the direct messages sent to you.

- ● **Favs.** Click to see the tweets you've marked as favorites.
- ● **Followers.** Click to see the people who follow you.
- ● **Following.** Click to see the users you follow.
- ● **Public.** Click to see what's happening in Twitter's public timeline.
- ● **Archive.** Click to see the tweets you've sent.

8.14 Click the Symbols tool to see this collection of tweet-enhancing characters.

Tweetree

Tweetree (http://tweetree.com/) isn't a full-featured Twitter replacement, but that's okay because it offers a few features that you won't find anywhere else. To see what I mean, log in using your Twitter username and password to get to your Tweetree home page, as shown in figure 8.15. You get the usual update text box at the top, followed by your friends' tweetstream. Each tweet has icons that enable you to reply, retweet, or mark the update as a favorite.

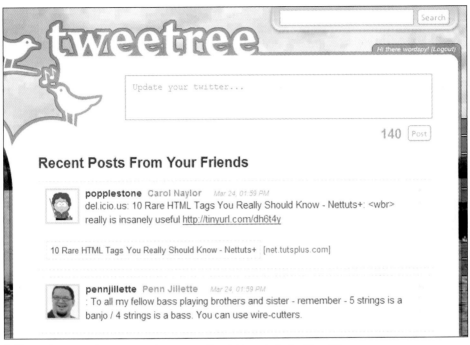

8.15 Your Tweetree home page shows your friends' tweets, but with a difference.

Here's where you notice the first of Tweetree's unique features (see the first tweet shown in figure 8.15). If a tweet includes a shortened URL, Tweetree automatically ferrets out the original Web address and displays the page title (as a link) and the domain where the page resides. Why bother? Two reasons:

- Many tweets introduce a shortened URL with only the barest of barebones descriptions: "Check this out doodz!!" or "This is funny LOL". Clicking the link more often than not wastes a few minutes of your precious time. By expanding the address automatically and showing the page title, you get a much better sense of what you're in for on the other side of the link.

- There's an inherent danger in a shortened URL because you simply don't know for sure where it will take you. Malicious users routinely use shortened URLs because they effectively hide the destination domain. With Tweetree, you not only see the domain, but you can hover your mouse over the link to see the full page address in the browser's status bar.

Either way, there's no more crossing of the fingers when you click a shortened URL.

I should mention, too, that Tweetree also looks for links to images on sites such as TwitPic and to videos on sites such as ffwd, and it automatically displays the media within the tweet, so you don't have to click yet another link to see yet another baby picture.

Finally, we come to the "tree" part of the Tweetree name. Tweetree examines your friends' tweets, and if it finds a reply, it grabs the original tweets and displays them using a tree-like format, as shown in figure 8.16. It's a nice way to listen in on a Twitter conversation.

8.16 Tweetree shows replies and their original tweets in a tree-like display.

Tweetvisor

Tweetvisor (http://tweetvisor.com/) is probably the most ambitious of the Web-based Twitter applications in that it doesn't compromise on features. Almost every bauble and bangle that you get on even the best desktop clients is available with Tweetvisor. The downside is that the interface is awfully busy, as you can see in figure 8.17.

8.17 Tweetvisor is a full-featured Twitter Web application.

Your Tweetvisor home page is chock full of stuff, so I'll just hit the highlights:

- **Your Replies.** This is the left column and it shows the reply tweets that folks have sent you. Click and drag the Set refresh rate slider to specify how often you want Tweetvisor to check for new replies.

- **Update box.** You use this box to send a tweet. It comes with a built-in URL shortener, and clicking the Tools link enables you to create tasks and shrink tweet text.

- **Tabs.** These are the buttons below the update box, and Tweetvisor offers nine in all, including Friends Timeline, Me (your tweets), Favorites, and Followers List. Click the Groups tab to create subsets of your friends. Click Search to run a Twitter search, which you can then save the search to the Favorite Searches tab by clicking the Save this topic and track the updates link. You can also click the Tweets About You tab to view a list of updates that mention you, or the RTs tab to see a list of updates that have retweeted your tweets.

- **Your Hot Topic.** This section is designed to show you the results of a Twitter search. If there's a topic you're particularly interested in monitoring, run a search using the Search tab, and then click the Make topic HOT link. This displays the result in the Your Hot Topic section, where Tweetvisor will update the results automatically every few minutes.

● **Friends Timeline.** This middle column shows your friends' tweets. Click Refresh to see more, or select the Real-time check box to have Tweetvisor refresh the timeline automatically. Hover your mouse over a tweet to see icons for replying, retweeting, sending a direct message, and marking the tweet as a favorite.

● **Your Direct Messages.** This column shows the direct messages that you've received.

Working with Twitter Gadgets and Widgets

If your desktop Twittering needs are fairly simple — you want to watch your friend's tweets go flying by, post an update every so often, and perhaps fire off the odd reply — then a big, fat desktop program or slow-to-load Web application isn't for you. Instead, you should consider a Twitter gadget or widget, a low-calorie application that lets you perform the basic Twitter tasks without getting in the way of your other activities.

Adding a Twitter gadget to your Windows Sidebar or desktop

If you're running Windows Vista, you may have the Windows Sidebar tucked into the right side of your monitor. Sidebar displays gadgets, which are mini-applications dedicated to some small task, such as displaying the weather. There are a few Twitter gadgets out there for Windows, so if you want to use one of them on your PC, follow these steps to download one:

Gadgets are also available for Windows 7, although that version of Microsoft's flagship operating system has done away with the Sidebar and displays all gadgets right on the desktop.

1. **First, make sure the Sidebar is displayed by choosing Start ⇨ All Programs ⇨ Accessories ⇨ Windows Sidebar.**

2. **Launch your favorite Web browser and use it to navigate to http://gallery.live. com/.** The Windows Live Gallery page appears.

3. **In the search box, type twitter and press Enter.** Windows Live Gallery displays all the gadgets that match your search term.

4. Click the Sidebar gadgets link. Windows Live Gallery displays all the Twitter gadgets, as shown in figure 8.18.

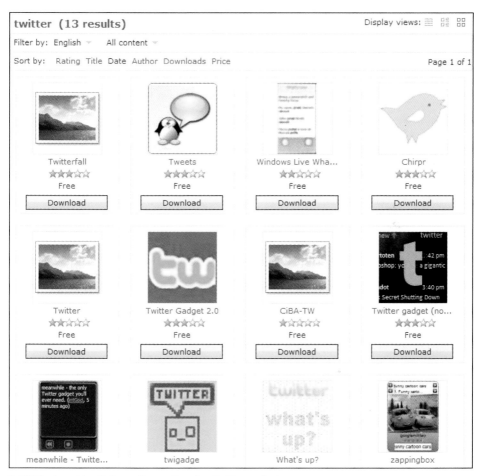

8.18 Windows Live Gallery offers quite a few Twitter gadgets.

5. Check out the gadgets by clicking the link under each gadget thumbnail. In the page that appears, you see a description of the gadget, user reviews, the number of downloads, and more. Use this information to select a gadget that suits you.

6. Display the page for your gadget of choice and click Download. Windows Live Gallery displays a warning that you should only install gadgets from developers you trust.

7. **Click Install.** The File Download dialog box appears.

8. **Click Open.** The Internet Explorer Security dialog box appears.

9. **Click Allow.** The Windows Sidebar - Security Alert dialog box appears. Grrr!

10. **Click Install.** Finally, your gadget appears in the Sidebar (or on the desktop in Windows 7).

11. **Configure your gadget with your Twitter credentials and whatever other options the gadget offers.** To configure a gadget, move the mouse pointer over the gadget, and then click the wrench icon (see figure 8.19).

Adding a Twitter widget to your Mac dashboard

If you want to do the Twitter thing using your Mac's Dashboard application, there's a widget called (not even remotely surprising) Twidget that's worth the download. Here's how to get it:

1. **Open Safari (or whatever Web browser you prefer) and direct it to www.apple.com/downloads/dashboard/.** The Dashboard Widgets page appears.

2. **In the Search box, type twidget.** The page displays a link to the Twidget widget.

3. **Click Twidget.** The download page for Twidget appears.

4. **Click Download.** Your browser downloads the widget and the Widget Installer appears.

5. **Click Install.** Within seconds, the Dashboard opens and you see Twidget ready and raring to go.

6. **Type your Twitter username and password and choose My Friends in the Timeline Display pop-up menu.**

8.19 A Twitter gadget alive and well in the Windows Sidebar

7. **Click Done.**

8. **Click Keep.** Figure 8.20 shows the Twidget widget running in the dashboard.

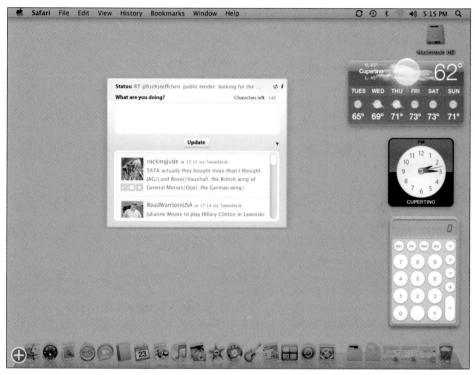

8.20 Twidget lets you post updates; monitor your friends' tweets; and replay, retweet, and favorite those tweets.

Adding a Twitter gadget to your iGoogle page

If you've got a customized iGoogle page loaded with gadgets, why not add a Twitter gadget into the mix? Here's how:

1. **Head directly to your iGoogle page by surfing to www.google.com/ig.**

2. **If you don't have an automatic sign-in, click Sign In, type your Google e-mail address and password, and then click Sign in.**

3. **Click the Add stuff link.** Google displays the Gadgets tab.

4. **In the Search for gadgets text box, type twitter and click Search.** Google displays a list of Twitter gadgets.

5. **Check out the gadgets by clicking the link for each gadget.** In the page that appears, you see a screen shot, a description of the gadget, user reviews, the number of downloads, and more. Use this information to select a gadget that suits you.

6. **Display the page for your preferred gadget and then click Add it now.** Google adds the gadget to your iGoogle home page.

7. **Click Back to iGoogle home.**

8. **Use the gadget to log in to your Twitter account.** Figure 8.21 shows TwitterGadget in my iGoogle home page.

8.21 You can tweet right from your iGoogle home page by adding a Twitter gadget.

Displaying tweets in Firefox

If you're a Firefox fan, you probably won't be surprised to know that you can customize the browser with Twitter-related extensions. These are mostly simple apps that show your friends' tweets and let you post updates. Here are the three most popular Twitter extensions for Firefox:

● **TwitterFox.** This extension (available from http://twitterfox.net/) adds a Twitter icon in the bottom-left corner of the Firefox window. After installing, click the icon to type your Twitter account credentials. TwitterFox looks for new tweets every five minutes and then lets you know when new updates arrive. Click the TwitterFox icon to see the tweets or post one of your own (see figure 8.22).

● **Power Twitter.** This extension (get it directly from the Mozilla Downloads page at https://addons.mozilla.org/en-US/firefox/addon/9591) is actually designed to enhance the Twitter.com site. Power Twitter adds new features to Twitter such as converting shortened URLs to their original addresses, showing images and videos within the tweet (see figure 8.23), adding buttons to share a photo and shorten a URL to the update box, adding a Search box in your sidebar, adding a retweet icon to each update, and integrating Twitter with Facebook.

8.22 Click the TwitterFox icon to see your incoming friend feed or post a tweet.

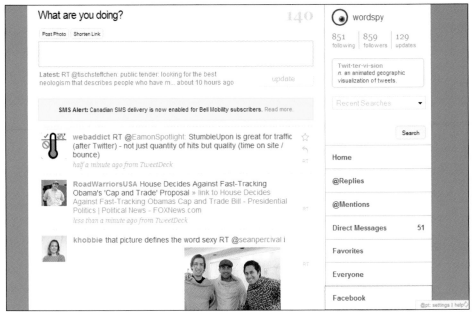

8.23 Power Twitter extends Twitter.com by adding inline images, de-shortening shortened URLs, and more.

 Some of Power Twitter's features only come alive if you give the extension your Twitter password. To do that, click the Settings link that appears in the lower-right corner of the screen.

- **TwitKit.** This extension (get it here: https://addons.mozilla.org/en-US/firefox/addon/6845) adds a sidebar to Firebox, as you can see in figure 8.24. It's a pretty standard Twitter client that enables you to post updates, see your friends' tweets (updated automatically; yes!); reply and favorite those tweets; and view lists of your friends, followers, replies, and tweets.

8.24 TwitKit is a Firefox sidebar extension that lets you work with your Twitter account.

What Tools Can I Use to Extend Twitter?

1 2 3 4 5 6 7 8 9

At its heart, Twitter is based on a refreshingly simple premise: you post short updates about what's happening in your life, follow your friends' updates, and create conversations around those updates. So it's more than a little odd that such a simple service would end up with this massive ecosystem of applications, Web sites, utilities, and other tools that aim to extend and enhance the basic Twitter experience. But the other idea at the heart of Twitter is openness, and making most profiles and tweets available to all comers has enabled the world's programming geniuses to come up with some eye-poppingly useful tools, as you see in this chapter.

Shortening URLs

Typing a tweet and watching the ubiquitous characters-you-have-left counter fall is like being in one of those movie scenarios where the walls of a room slowly close in on the hero. The closer you get to zero, the more tense you feel, and the more pressure there is to escape before it's too late!

One of the more common Twitter conundrums occurs when you write an admirably concise-but-coherent tweet, see that you've still got 25 or so characters to spare, breathe a sigh of relief, and then realize you still have to include a 75-character Web address. Doh! The solution is to knock that address down to size using a URL-shortening service. This is a Web site (usually; there are programs and plug-ins available, too) that accepts any Web address, no matter how long, and reduces it to a much shorter URL that's almost always less than two dozen characters (and often under 20).

For example, consider the following address (this book's Amazon.com page, actually):

```
http://www.amazon.com/Twitter-Tips-Tricks-Tweets-McFedries/dp/0470529695/
```

This is a 73-character address, which isn't super long by modern Web standards, but it would still use up over half your tweet allotment. When I ran this address through the URL-shortening machine at bit.ly (http://bit.ly/), I ended up with this:

```
http://bit.ly/ieXOl
```

The bit.ly service (like all URL shorteners) generates a random string of letters and numbers (usually five characters, but sometimes as few as four), and associates the resulting short address with the original address. When someone surfs to the shortened URL, bit.ly (or whatever) looks up the associated original URL and then redirects the Web browser to that address. Best of all, because the shortened address consists of (in this case) a mere 19 characters, you've just awarded yourself an extra 54 characters to (in this case) praise the book!

The clash between the immovable object of Twitter's 140-character limit and the irresistible force of people tweeting links to interesting and fun Web sites has created a boom in the URL-shortening business. Hundreds of services have sprung up, seemingly overnight, and it's now quite the cottage industry. That's great, but how on Earth are you supposed to choose which service to use?

In some cases the answer is you don't have to. Many third-party Twitter tools come with built-in connections to URL shorteners, so you just type your address, click Shorten (or whatever), and away you go. Some, like TweetDeck and twhirl, actually offer multiple shortening services, which narrows things down, but still forces you to make a choice. If you don't like any of the services offered, or if you use the Twitter Web site to post and so don't have direct access to URL shortening, then you must find your own.

The Twitter Web site doesn't have a URL-shortening feature on its interface, but it does shorten URLs. If you post a tweet that includes a regular Web address, Twitter will often shorten that address using the TinyURL service (http://tinyurl.com/).

To help you decide, here are a few things to look for in a URL-shortening service:

- **Short domain name.** This is probably the most important and the most obvious trait to look for. Clearly a service named, say, getyoururlshortenedheredude.com just isn't going to help all that much. The best sites have truly tiny domain names, from tinyurl.com (ironically, one of the longer names in this field) to is.gd (a five-character domain name such as this is the shortest possible name).

- **Custom short code.** The four- and five-character codes generated by URL-shortening services aren't particularly memorable or informative. One of the signs of a good shortener is that it gives you the option to specify your own code. For example, if you want to share a link to your cubic zirconia jewelry auction on eBay, you could use, say, TinyURL to create a short address that's easy to remember (for example, http://tinyurl.com/cubicz) or informative (for example, http://tinyurl.com/CubicZirconiaAuction).

- **Link preview.** Many people are paranoid about shortened URLs because they give no indication of what lurks on the business end of the link. Hackers who have gone over to the dark side of the force often use short URLs to lure the unsuspecting into malicious sites. Less darkly, the site could be one known for excessive pop-ups, overuse of Flash and other media, or other annoying features. A good URL-shortening service will offer some way for users to preview the original address before actually going there. For example, is.gd (http://is.gd/) lets you preview a link by adding a hyphen (-) after the shortened URL.

- **Statistics.** How do you know if people are clicking your tweet links like crazy or ignoring them with a vengeance? The truth is, you don't. You may be able to tease some numbers out of your Web server log if you're linking to your own site (which just sounds like way too much work), and you're completely in the dark when it comes to links to other sites. Many URL-shortening services offer link statistics (they often call them *analytics*) that tell you (at the very least) how many times your short URL has been used. Stat geeks love sites such as cli.gs (http://cli.gs/) that offer reams of numbers: total hits, hits by day, hits by country, and more.

With all that in mind, here are a half dozen URL-shortening services to consider:

- **TinyURL** (http://tinyurl.com/). This is one of the oldest and best known services, and it's currently by far the most popular, mostly thanks to its current position as Twitter's default URL-shortening service. It offers custom short codes and a link preview option (using the domain preview.tinyurl.com).

- **bit.ly** (http://bit.ly/). This service is becoming very popular, mostly thanks to its short domain name and its setting as the default shortening service in TweetDeck. It offers custom short codes, and if you sign up for a free account, you link stats that show total clicks, clicks by country, date, and more (see figure 9.1). You can also post a tweet right from the bit.ly site!

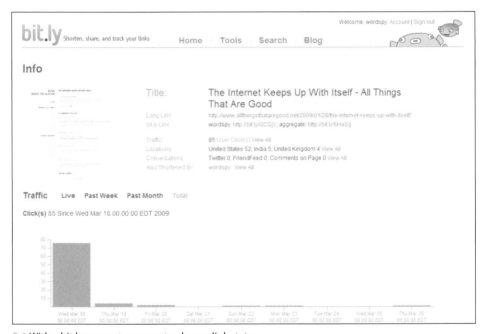

9.1 With a bit.ly account, you can track your link stats.

- **is.gd** (http://is.gd/). This service (it's pronounced "is good") is gaining ground in the URL shortening race mostly because it uses the minimum five-character domain and its short codes are only four characters, so a total is.gd short URL grabs just 17 characters of precious tweet real estate. You give users a link preview by adding a hyphen (-) to the end of the short URL, so adding the feature takes up only a single extra character. is.gd doesn't offer custom codes or statistics as I write this.

● **tr.im** (http://tr.im). I like this service because the name is both apropos ("trim"!) and maximally short, not to mention the short codes are just four characters. You can specify custom short codes, and if you create an account, you get stats for each URL (see figure 9.2), which include hits by country, referring Web sites, browser, and operating system. And if you create a tr.im account using the same username and password as your Twitter account, you can shorten a URL and post it to Twitter all in one fell swoop.

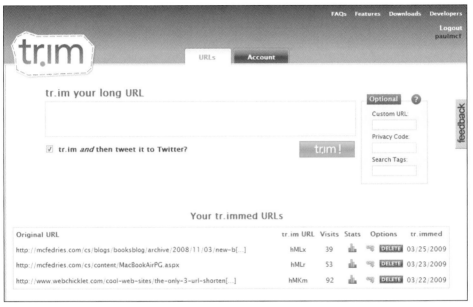

9.2 If you create a tr.im account, you can track link visits and other stats.

● **twurl.nl** (http://twurl.nl/). This is the service used by Tweetburner (http://tweetburner. com/), which offers extensive link statistics when you sign up for a Feedburner account. No custom short codes, however, and no preview feature.

● **cli.gs** (http://cli.gs/). This service has most of the basics, including a short domain and custom short codes. However, its forte is data, lots and lots of data. You can track not only hits, but hits by country and by social network, and you can even create separate URLs for different services (for example, one for Twitter and one for Facebook).

Having trouble shoehorning your text into a tweet? Then consider using the TweetShrink service (http://tweetshrink.com/), which trims text by converting certain words to short forms.

Sharing Photos, Videos, and Music

Facebook users get to share photos and videos with their friends, and MySpace users also get to share their favorite MySpace bands with their peeps. Twitter is, obviously, a text-only medium, so sharing media with your tweeps is out, right? True, you can't embed media directly into a tweet, but you can embed links to any media that you've added to other sites, such as Flickr and YouTube.

That works, but the entire process is a bit on the exhausting side, particularly if you want to share lots of stuff:

1. Go to the site where your media is hosted.

2. Upload the media to the site.

3. Copy the address of the page that displays the media.

4. Go to a URL-shortening service and shorten the address from step 3.

5. Go to Twitter or load your favorite Twitter application.

6. Compose a tweet about the media, paste the shortened URL, and then fire away.

My but that's an awfully roundabout way to perform a task that takes only a few mouse clicks on Facebook or MySpace. Ah, but the Twitterverse can be remarkably resourceful when it senses something missing from its vast toolbox. So now there are special Twitter-friendly sites where you can perform all of these steps in one place. It's the civilized way to share photos, videos, and music. The next few sections tell you about a few of these sites.

Sharing photos

If a picture is worth a thousand words, then a single photo is the equivalent of about seven tweets! Fortunately, you only have to post a single tweet to share a photo using any of the many photo-sharing services that support Twitter. In the next section, I show you how to TwitPic and later I give you some info about a few other photo-sharing sites.

How nice would it be to view photos within your tweets rather than having to click to another site? Really nice! Happily, we're starting to see this feature — usually called *inline photos* — added to more Twitter applications. For example, the iPhone app Twittelator Pro (see Chapter 5) displays inline photos, as do the Web sites Tweetree and the Firefox plug-in Power Twitter (both described in Chapter 8).

Using TwitPic

The gold standard in photo sharing for Twitter is TwitPic (http://twitpic.com/), which is by far the most popular photo sharing service for tweeters. This is partly because almost every Twitter application that comes with some sort of "Share a photo" feature uses TwitPic to handle the dirty work of uploading the photo and shortening the URL. However, the TwitPic site itself is really easy to use, and you can even use TwitPic to upload photos by e-mail (from your camera phone, for example).

Here's the procedure to follow to upload a photo and post a tweet using the TwitPic site:

1. **Navigate to http://twitpic.com/ and type your Twitter account username and password.** Your TwitPic home page appears. The photos you post will appear here.

2. **Click Upload photo.** The Upload and post a photo page appears.

3. **Click Browse.** (If you're using a Mac, click Choose File.) The Choose File to Upload dialog box appears.

4. **Choose the photo you want to upload and then click Open (or click Choose on your Mac).**

5. **Type a message to go along with your photo, as shown in figure 9.3.**

9.3 With TwitPic, you choose a photo, write a message, and then ship the tweet.

6. **Click Upload.** TwitPic uploads the photo, shortens the photo's URL, and then posts that address and your message as a tweet (see figure 9.4).

paulmcf

🔒 http://twitpic.com/2fish - This is my favorite picture of Gypsy!

less than 20 seconds ago from TwitPic

🔒 http://twitpic.com/2fiec - Gypsy in the snow
12 minutes ago from TwitPic

🔒 http://twitpic.com/2fhnk - Now "that" is a good-looking dog!
37 minutes ago from TwitPic

9.4 TwitPic takes care of shortening the photo URL and posting the URL and your message to your Twitter account.

note TwitPic also lets you tweet a photo from your mobile phone. In your TwitPic page, click Settings to see your special TwitPic address, which takes the form *username. pin*@twitpic.com, where *username* is your Twitter screen name, and *pin* is a four-digit number (which you can change). E-mail a photo to that address from your phone (your subject line is the tweet text), and it appears as a tweet a few minutes later.

Other photo sharing services

TwitPic may be the Big Kahuna of Twitter photo-sharing services, but it's not the only game in that particular town. Here are a few others to check out:

- **Mobypicture** (http://mobypicture.com/). This service lets you share photos not only with Twitter, but with a wide variety of sites, including Facebook, Flickr, Jaiku, and blogging platforms such as WordPress and Blogger. For these other sites you have to create a Mobypicture account, but for Twitter, you don't need to create a new account (unless you want to, of course); instead, you log in using your Twitter credentials. You can then upload your photos using the Web site, via e-mail, MMS (multimedia messaging service), or the Mobypicture iPhone app.

- **Pikchur** (http://pikchur.com/). This site also supports a wide variety of sites, including Facebook, FriendFeed, identi.ca, tumblr, and many more. On the login page, be sure to choose Twitter from the list, and then type your Twitter account credentials. Once you're in, you can upload via the Web site or set up an e-mail address to post from your phone using e-mail or MMS.

- **SnapTweet** (http://snaptweet.com/). If you have a Flickr (www.flickr.com) account, you can use SnapTweet to post tweets that link to your Flickr photos. Sign in to SnapTweet using your Twitter account username and password, along with your Flickr address. You'll see your latest Flickr photo, and you can start uploading.

- **Visual Twitter** (http://visualtwitter.com/). This service lets you post photo tweets via e-mail using your mobile phone. Log in using your Twitter account credentials, click Setup, and then enter your mobile phone number. Once your phone number is confirmed, you can send photo tweets by e-mailing a photo to me@visualtwitter.com.

- **yfrog** (http://yfrog.com/). This site presents a simple interface (see figure 9.5) that lets you upload either a local photo or a photo on the Web. Type a message, enter your Twitter username and password, and then click Post it! to send the tweet. One of the nice features of yfrog is that when people click the link to load your photo, the yfrog page include a (Re)Tweet this image link that enables tweeters to easily retweet your photo. The yfrog site is also optimized for the iPhone, and pointing mobile Safari to yfrog.com displays the interface shown in figure 9.6.

9.5 The yfrog site lets you upload local or Web-based images and post a link as a tweet.

Sharing videos

Although photo sharing is the type of media most often shared by tweeters, video is right up there, as well. That's not surprising given the immense popularity of YouTube and other video sharing sites. Here are four Web sites that make it easy to share video with your Twitter tribe:

9.6 The yfrog site is iPhone-friendly.

- **ffwd** (www.ffwd.com). This interesting site lets you build a personal list of *channels*, which can be TV shows, Web-based video shows, and more. Once you add a channel to your account, you browse through its video offerings, and when you come across something you want to share, you click the Share on Twitter icon, sign in to your Twitter account, and then post the update. For faster service, you can add your Twitter credentials to your profile (click Profile and then click Account).

- **TweeTube** (http://tweetube.com/). This site is designed to help you easily share YouTube videos with your Twitter posse. The home page includes a text box that you use to paste the address of the YouTube video you want to feature (you can also use the TweeTube site to search for YouTube videos). Click Get Video and TweeTube retrieves the video, as shown in figure 9.7. Type a message, type your Twitter account username and password, and then click Share this video.

- **Twiddeo** (http://twiddeo.com/). This new service lets you upload and share your own video with your tweeps. You can upload a video file from your computer, beam in a video captured on your phone, or even record a video straight from your Web cam.

● **TwitWall** (http://twitwall.com/). This site enables you to share not only videos, but also images and music files. Log in with your Twitter account credentials, click Add an Entry, and then specify a message and your video specifics. For the latter, click the Embed Tags tab and then your video code (such as the <object> tag code associated with a YouTube video).

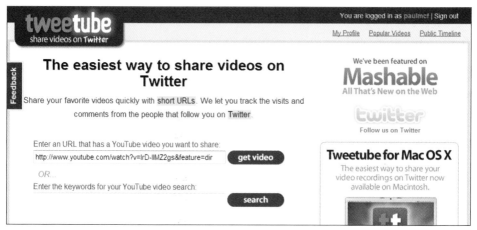

9.7 TweeTube makes it easy to share YouTube videos with your Twitter pals.

Want to sample the videos that tweeters around the world are sharing with their friends? You could search Twitter for "video," and wade through all the nonvideo results, or you can take a trip to Twitmatic (http://twitmatic.com/), which dips into the stream of public timeline videos and lets you see what's being shared. Prepare to waste lots of time on this site!

Sharing music

Got a favorite song you'd like to share? That's awfully nice of you. Fortunately, sharing a tune on Twitter is easy if you use any of the following music sharing sites:

● **Blip.fm** (http://blip.fm/). This site lets you set up your own broadcast station. Create an account and then configure it to share with Twitter by typing your Twitter credentials. Locate a song from the Blip.FM archives, click Blip, type some text to appear in your tweet, and then click OK.

- **Song.ly** (http://song.ly/). This site is a combination music search service and music sharing service. Type an artist or song title and click Search, and Song.ly looks for matching music on the Web. In the results (see figure 9.8), if you see the song you want to share, click the Tweet icon, sign in to your Twitter account, and then post the tweet.

- **Twiturm** (http:/twiturm.com/). You can use this site to share your own music by uploading an MP3 file, or to share Web-based MP3s by specifying a song's Web address. Log in with your Twitter username and password, and then click Upload. Specify a local file or a Web address, type a message for the tweet, and then click Upload.

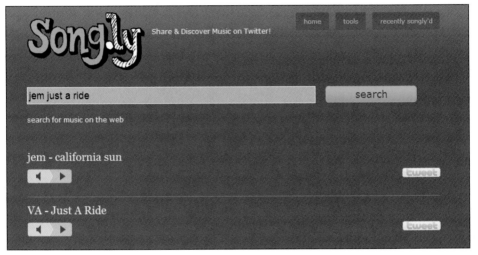

9.8 You can use Song.ly to search for music on the Web and then share it on Twitter.

- **twt.fm** (http://.twt.fm/). This site is by far the most popular music sharing service among Twitter users. Twt.fm associated with IMEEM (http://imeem.com/), so it has access to the millions of songs in the IMEEM database, but twt.fm can also locate music streams on the Web or share your MP3 links. The home page asks for your Twitter username, an artist name, and a track name. Click Preview and, if twt.fm finds the track (see figure 9.9), click Yes! Tweet It to switch to Twitter where you can post the tweet.

 If your friends only share music occasionally, you can wait quite a while between music tweets, or you could miss a music tweet. Fortunately, you can use Twisten.fm (http://twisten.fm/) to cull just the music tweets from your friend timeline. Log in using your Twitter username and password, and Twisten.FM displays a Following list that displays the music shared recently by your friends. Click the Everyone list to see music being shared on the public timeline.

9.9 The twt.fm site has an uncanny ability to find almost any song and then let you share it with your Twitter sidekicks.

Posting to Multiple Social Networks

It's becoming increasingly rare these days to find anyone who can make do with just a single social network. Most of us have two or three or more groups of online friends that we pester with status updates, but logging in to each site and firing off a message just gets too time-consuming. Fortunately, the world's programmers must also be social butterflies because they've come up with a few useful solutions that let you post a status update (and sometimes a photo or video, too) to multiple social networks.

Here are a few examples:

- **HelloTxt** (http://hellotxt.com/)
- **Socialthing** (http://socialthing.com/)
- **Twitterfeed** (http://twitterfeed.com/)

However, the most popular service among the over-networked set right now is Ping.fm, which currently supports 39 social networks, and seems to add new ones on a scarily regular basis. (I don't know about you, but I didn't even know there were 39 social networks until I joined Ping.fm!) These networks include all the major online hangouts, including Facebook, MySpace, Friendster, del.icio.us, Flickr, Jaiku, and, of course, Twitter.

That's impressive enough, but Ping.fm also raises eyebrows with its incredible variety of posting options: e-mail, mobile phone, SMS, MMS, instant messaging (AIM, Yahoo! Messenger, Google Talk, and Windows Live Messenger), gadgets (such as Ping.fm for iGoogle), Web applications (such as Twitterfeed (http://twitterfeed.com/) and the Ping.fm application on Facebook), and desktop applications (such as twhirl).

Getting started with Ping.fm

Your first chore is to sign up, which you can do by following these steps:

1. **Make a beeline with your browser for http://ping.fm/.**

2. **Click Signup.**

3. **Type your e-mail address and a password (twice).**

4. **Click Signup.** Ping.fm creates your account and displays the Manage Social Networks page, shown in figure 9.10.

9.10 When you first sign up with Ping.fm, you see the Manage Social Networks page with its incredible list of social networks supported by Ping.fm.

The idea is that you run through the list of social networks, and for each one you use, click the Add Network link and set up your account particulars. Here are the steps to follow for configuring Twitter on Ping.fm:

1. **On the Manage Social Networks page, click the Add Network link beside Twitter.**
   The Settings / Twitter page appears, as shown in figure 9.11.

Settings / Twitter

Fill in your Twitter login information below. If you don't have a Twitter account, you should probably get one before filling out this form.

Click here to get your Twitter account. It's free!

Username: paulmcf	Use for: ☑ Status updates ☑ Micro-blogging
Password: ••••••••••	Extras: ☑ Update location (what?)
Submit Cancel	

9.11 Use the Settings / Twitter page to configure your Twitter account on Ping.fm.

2. **Type your Twitter username and password.**
3. **Leave the Status updates check box and the Micro-blogging check box selected.**
4. **If you plan on posting to Ping.fm using a device with built-in GPS (such as an iPhone 3G) and you want Ping.fm to modify your Twitter location data, leave the Update location check box selected.**
5. **Click Submit.**

To add more networks, click Dashboard at the top of any Ping.fm page, then click the Add More Networks link in the Social Networks section of the Dashboard page.

Getting your Ping.fm application key

If you plan on using Ping.fm with third-party applications such as twhirl (see the next section), iGoogle, or Facebook, then you need to provide those applications with your Ping.fm application key. Here's what you do:

1. **Click Dashboard at the top of any Ping.fm page.** The Your Dashboard page appears.

2. **In the Services / Tools section, click Application Keys.** The Application Keys page appears.

3. **Click the Desktop / Web Key value.** Ping.fm automatically copies the key.

4. **Open the third-party program, access the Ping.fm application, gadget, or whatever, and then paste the application key when prompted.**

Configuring twhirl to use Ping.fm

If you use twhirl (which I talked about in Chapter 8) to post to Twitter, you can also use it to pass along your tweets to Ping.fm. Here's how:

1. **In twhirl, click Configuration (the wrench icon).** The Configuration dialog box opens.

2. **Display the General tab.**

3. **Select the Ping.fm check box.**

4. **Type your Ping.fm app key.**

5. **Click Save.** twhirl saves your new settings, and will now also send your tweets to your Ping.fm account.

Posting with Ping.fm

Posting a status update with Ping.fm is this easy:

1. **Click Dashboard at the top of any Ping.fm page.** The Your Dashboard page appears.

2. **Use the Ping My list to decide where you want the message to go:**

   - If you want to update all your networks that accept status updates (including Twitter), either leave the Default item chosen, or choose Statuses.

   - If you only want to send the update to a single network (such as Twitter), choose that network in the list.

The Ping.fm Default setting is usually Statuses, meaning that a ping gets sent to networks that accept status updates. To check this, click Settings, click Default Settings, and then choose Status Updates in the Default method list.

3. **Type your message in the large text box.**

4. **Click Ping it.**

More Twitter Tools to Play With

The Twitterverse is so crowded with Twitter-related tools that it would take another book this size, heck another two books this size to cover them all. I might just do that one day, but for now I'll delve into a few tools that I think are useful, fun, or just plain cool.

Scheduling tweets

Sometimes you compose a tweet, but then realize it would be better if you posted it later. For example, it could be a birthday greeting or other message to a friend in a different time zone who, if you sent it now, might miss it because she's sleeping. Or perhaps you're going on vacation for a week and, not being a Twitterholic, you decide to also take a week off from tweeting. However, you don't want your account to appear dormant, so it would be nice to compose a few tweets now, and then have them posted every day or two while you're away.

Yes, Twitter is all about what's happening now, but sometimes your life is about what's happening then. For those times, you can take advantage of the growing list of services that let you schedule tweets. Here's a sampling:

- **FutureTweets** (http://futuretweets.com). With this service you can publish a tweet at a specific date and time, or you can set up a recurring tweet that gets shipped out daily, weekly, monthly, or yearly. Also includes the completely unrelated capability of flipping tweet text upside down and backwards. No, I don't know why.

- **HootSuite** (http://hootsuite.com). This service lets you send tweets now or at a specified date and time. You can set up multiple Twitter accounts and perform most basic Twitter functions (send replies, retweets, and direct messages, unfollow people, see the replies and directs you've received, and more).

- **TweetLater** (www.tweetlater.com). The free version of this service lets you post tweets a specific number of minutes, hours, days, or weeks from now, or at a specific date and time (see figure 9.12). TweetLater Professional (for which you must fork over a monthly fee) lets you create recurring tweets. Both versions also include many other tools for managing your Twitter life, including multiple Twitter accounts, automatic follows and unfollows, keyword tracking, and more.

There's nothing wrong with scheduling tweets, but it's probably not something you want to overdo. There's an oddly impersonal quality to the whole exercise, so it feels sort of like getting your assistant to buy your spouse's birthday present.

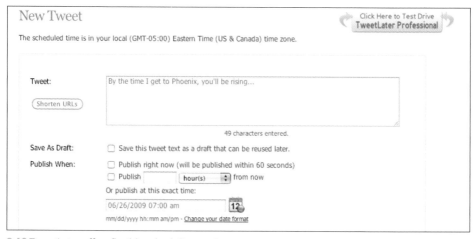

9.12 TweetLater offers flexible scheduling options, so you can tweet now, minutes, hours, days, or weeks from now, or at a date and time that suits you.

Following Twitter trends

As a source of information, your everyday experience with Twitter probably consists of reading your friends' incoming tweets, and perhaps occasionally tuning in to the public timeline to marvel at the confusion and sheer incomprehensibility of it all. Looking at Twitter tweet-by-tweet it all seems so random, like so many atoms whooshing by.

However, just as atoms have a genius for combining into tangible objects, so too does the tweetstream produce its own order out of chaos. I'm talking here about Twitter trends, those topics and ideas that suddenly, without anyone planning anything or controlling anything, seem to be on everyone's Twitter lips.

Twitter itself mines the vast public database of tweets for interesting trends, and displays the top ten on the Twitter Search page (see Chapter 6). Of course, Twitter programmers want in on this action, too, so there's no shortage of tools that let you get a sense of the Twitter zeitgeist. Here are just a few to get you started:

- **Tweetmeme** (www.tweetmeme.com). This site examines the links in the tweetstream and shows which ones have been tweeted most often (see figure 9.13).

- **Twist** (http://twist.flaptor.com). You can use this site to see how often a particular topic has been mentioned on Twitter, and you can even compare two or more topics.

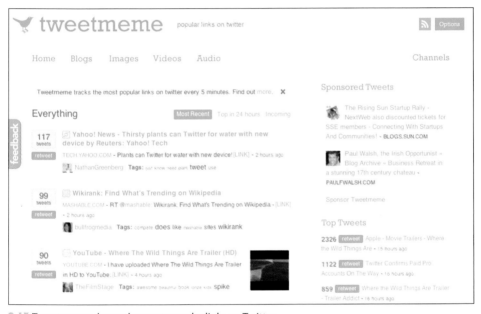

9.13 Tweetmeme shows the most popular links on Twitter.

- **TwitScoop** (www.twitscoop.com). This addictive site offers a Buzzing right now feature that shows the most popular Twitter topics in a cloud format, where the more popular a topic is, the larger and bolder its text (see figure 9.14). The addictiveness comes from the real-time display that shows topics growing and shrinking as you watch.

- **Twopular** (http://twopular.com). This site shows you the trending Twitter topics in different timeframes: the past two hours, eight hours, day, week, month, and ever since the service began (in late 2008). One nice touch is the use of up, down, and sideways arrows to indicate a trend's direction.

9.16 The twittearth site displays real-time tweets in 3-D.

A similar site is Twittervision (http://twittervision.com/), which offers both 2-D and 3-D maps of real-time tweets.

Getting your Twitter account ranking

When a site turns up near the top of a Google search, that site is said to have lots of *Googlejuice*. So if your Twitter account is getting lots of buzz (followers, retweets, shoutouts, whatever), then I guess you could say that it's got lots of *Twitterjuice*. How would you know for sure, though? You could just go with what your gut tells you, but if you want something a bit less subjective, then I suggest you check out any of the following sites, which can tell you where you stand in the overall Twitter scheme of things:

- **TwinFluence** (http://twinfluence.com/). This site offers several interesting statistics that aim to measure your influence within the Twitterverse (see figure 9.17). The top number is your overall influence rank and its percentile. Besides basic friends and followers numbers, you also get stats for your second-order followers (the total number of people your followers follow); velocity (the rate at which your account is accumulating second-order followers); social capital (the average number of followers that your followers have); and centralization (a measure of how much of your total number of second-order followers is dependent on a few people with high followerships). There's lots of good math meat here if you have a taste for that kind of thing.

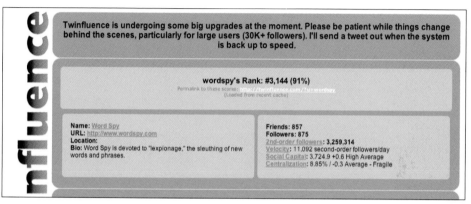

9.17 Find out how much influence you have in the twitosphere with Twinfluence.

- **Twitalyzer** (http://twitalyzer.com/). This site analyzes your overall influence in Twitter circles using five measures: signal-to-noise ratio (where *signal* refers to tweets that pass on information such as links and retweets, and *noise* refers to everything else); generosity (how often you retweet); velocity (the relative rate at which you post tweets); and clout (the relative rate at which other people reference your account in their tweets).

- **TwitterCounter** (http://twittercounter.com). This site shows your total number of followers and a graph of your followership growth over the past week. It also calculates the number of new followers you get per day and predicts how many you'll have in 30 days.

- **Twitter Grader** (http://twitter.grader.com/). This site delves deep into your Twitter data to provide you with an overall number that's supposed to show where you rank against all other Twitter users. The site offers no clue as to how this rank is calculated, so take the results with one or two grains of salt.

Displaying your latest tweet on a photo

SayTweet (http://saytweet.com/) qualifies as a tool if by the word tool you mean "a silly, pointless, but just plain fun mashup that you can display on your Web site." The idea is that you upload a photo (or provide a photo URL) to SayTweet, click that photo, and then provide your Twitter username. At the spot you clicked, SayTweet adds a speech bubble, and your most recent tweet appears in that bubble. The site then provides you with some code to add to your site, and visitors see your photo and speech-bubble tweet, as shown in figure 9.18. Silly? Check. Pointless? Check. Just plain fun? Check.

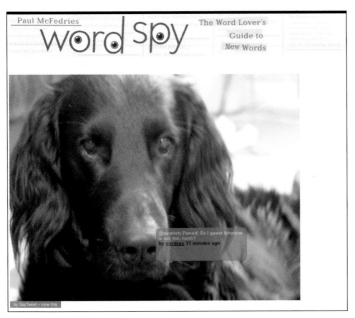

9.18 Use SayTweet to display your latest tweet in a speech bubble on a photo. Why not?

Tweeting events to your Google calendar

Do you keep your life running smoothly by using Google Calendar (http://google.calendar.com/) to track your appointments, meetings, three-martini lunches, and other events? If so, you'll be happy to know that you can also keep your life running smoothly from the Twittersphere by taking advantage of a tool that lets you update Google Calendar via Twitter.

Twittercal (http://twittercal.com/) is a service that lets you update your Google Calendar using a direct message on Twitter. You follow @gcal on Twitter, provide Twittercal with your Twitter username and Gmail address, and then authorize Twittercal to access your Google Calendar.

When all that's done, you send a direct message to @gcal to add events to your calendar. You use Google Calendar's Quick Add syntax, which is described in glorious detail here:

http://www.google.com/support/calendar/bin/answer.py?answer=36604

For example, figure 9.19 shows a direct message designed to create a 15-minute-long event at 3:00PM today. Figure 9.20 shows the event safely scheduled in my calendar.

Direct message gcal:

d gcal Call Karen today at 3:00 pm for 15 minutes

Latest: I got a good chuckle from this Betty comic: http://comics.com/betty/200... less than 5 seconds ago

send

9.19 With Twittercal, you schedule Google Calendar events by sending direct messages to @gcal.

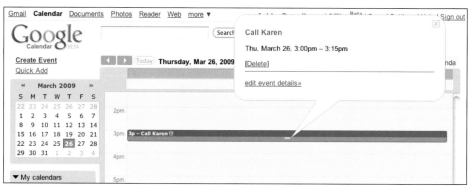

9.20 The event shown in figure 9.19 added to Google Calendar

Using LinkedIn to track tweets about your company

If you have a LinkedIn account (www.linkedin.com), you probably find it a useful tool for making new business contacts. However, you can also use it to track tweets that mention your company.

Sign on to LinkedIn and click Applications. Click the Company Buzz application to open the preview page, and then click Add application. Company Buzz automatically adds topics that cover your LinkedIn profile data, such as your company name, the names of previous employers, and your school names. You can also add other topics to track then within LinkedIn.

Send your blog feed to Twitter

If you've got a blog as well as a Twitter account, you can send a tweet each time you post a new blog entry to let your followers know you've got some outside content for them to read. However, why bother with that extra step when you can get your blog post sent automatically to your

233

Twitter account? The tool for this task is Twitterfeed (http://twitterfeed.com/), which takes items in from an RSS feed and automatically forwards them to a Twitter account.

Here's how you set things up:

1. **Go to http://twitterfeed.com/ and create an account.**

2. **Click Create new feed. Twitterfeed displays the Create new feed page.**

3. **In the Create new feed list, choose Twitter.**

4. **Use the Username and Password text boxes to enter your Twitter credentials.** At this point it's a good idea to click Test Twitter authentication to make sure Twitterfeed can connect to your Twitter account.

5. **Type the address of your blog's feed in the RSS Feed URL text box.** To make sure all's well, I suggest clicking Test RSS feed to ensure that Twitterfeed is receiving the feed loud and clear.

6. **Use the Update frequency list to choose how often you want Twitterfeed to check your RSS feed for new entries.**

7. **Use the Include list to choose what parts of each blog post you want posted to Twitter.** Choose Title & description, Title only, or Description only.

 Because tweets are limited to 140 characters and most blogs posts are much larger than that, the Title only option is usually the way to go here.

8. **If you don't want your update to include a link back to your blog, deselect the Include item link check box.**

9. **If you want to mark these tweets to indicate they come from your blog (for example, "Blog Post:"), type up to 20 characters in the Prefix each tweet with text box.** Figure 9.21 shows a complete feed ready for action.

10. **Click Create.** Twitterfeed creates your new feed.

Twitterfeed checks your blog feed after whatever time interval you chose in step 6, and it then posts your most recent blog entry to your Twitter account.

Create new [twitter ⬍] feed

Username: [paulmcf]   **Password**: [••••••••]   test twitter authentication
✔ twitter username and password OK

RSS Feed URL: [http://mcfedries.com/cs/blogs/booksblog/rss.aspx]   test rss feed
✔ Feed was parsed successfully

Update frequency: [Every 24 hours ⬍]   **Post up to** [1 ⬍] **new updates each time**
[Update Frequency describes how often we check your feed for new posts. The very first time we check, we post the most recent entry only, and after that, any new entries since the last time we checked.]

Include ... [title only   ⬍]
☑ Include item link (if unchecked, sends tweet without the link)   Shorten link through [TinyURL   ⬍]

Post new items based on [pubDate ⬍]

Prefix each tweet with: [Blog Post:]   (max. 20 characters)

Filter by keywords: [no filter]

☑ Active (if unchecked, this twitterfeed will be inactive, and will not post to twitter)

(Create) Cancel

9.21 Twitterfeed lets you send an RSS feed to your Twitter account.

glossary

avatar The user icon associated with a Twitter account.

badge A small graphic with a Twitter-inspired design that you use as a link to your Twitter home page.

bot An automated Twitter account that returns some kind of data in response to a specially formatted message.

celebritweet A celebrity or famous person who uses Twitter.

direct To send a direct message to someone; a direct message.

direct message A private note that only the recipient can read.

exactotweet See twoosh.

fail whale The page that Twitter displays when it is over capacity and can't accept any more tweets.

followership The people who follow a particular Twitter user.

followorthy Worthy of being followed on Twitter.

hashtag A word that, when preceded by a hash (#), defines or references a topic on Twitter.

hypertweeting Posting an excessive number of tweets.

live-tweeting Sending on-the-fly updates that describe or summarize some ongoing event.

mashup Information created by combining data from two or more different sources.

meme A cultural artifact, such as an idea or catchphrase, that spreads quickly from person to person.

microblogging Posting short thoughts and ideas to an online site such as Twitter.

mutual follow When two people on Twitter follow each other.

nudge A text message sent to your phone to remind you to post an update.

partial retweet A retweet that includes only part of the original tweet.

reply A response to a tweeter's update.

retweet Another person's tweet that you copy and send out to your followers, along with an acknowledgment of the original tweeter.

RT An abbreviation used to mark an update as a retweet; a retweet.

timeline A related collection of tweets, sorted by the date and time they were posted.

tweeple People who use Twitter.

tweeps A Twitter user's friends.

tweet An update posted to Twitter.

tweet cred Twitter credibility.

tweeter A person who uses Twitter.

tweetstream The tweets in a timeline.

tweetup A real-world meeting between two or more people who know each other through the online Twitter service.

tweetwalking Writing and posting a Twitter update while walking.

tweme A Twitter meme.

tweople See tweeple.

Twitosphere See Twitterverse.

Twittaholic A person who uses Twitter compulsively.

Twitterer A Twitter user.

Twitterati The Twitter users with the most followers and influence.

Twitterpated Overwhelmed by incoming tweets.

Twitterrhea The act of posting an excessive number of tweets in a short time.

Twittersphere See Twitterverse.

Twitterverse The Twitter social networking service and the people who use it.

Twitterstream See tweetstream.

Twitticism A witty tweet.

Twittiquette Twitter etiquette; an informal set of guidelines and suggestions for updating, following, replying, and sending direct messages.

twoosh A tweet that is exactly 140 characters long.

tword A new word created by appending "tw" to an existing word.

URL shortening service A Web site or program that converts a Web address into a much shorter URL and then uses that URL to redirect users to the original address.

Notes

index

The Genius is in.

Macs
PORTABLE GENIUS

978-0-470-29052-1

Mac OS X Leopard
PORTABLE GENIUS

978-0-470-29050-7

iPhone 3G
PORTABLE GENIUS

978-0-470-42348-6

Final Cut Pro
PORTABLE GENIUS

978-0-470-38760-3

iMac
PORTABLE GENIUS

978-0-470-29061-3

MacBook Air
PORTABLE GENIUS

978-0-470-38108-3

MacBook
PORTABLE GENIUS

978-0-470-29169-6

MacBook Pro
PORTABLE GENIUS

978-0-470-29170-2

The essentials for every forward-thinking Apple user are now available on the go. Designed for easy access to tools and shortcuts, the *Portable Genius* series has all the information you need to maximize your digital lifestyle. With a full-color interior and easy-to-navigate content, the *Portable Genius* series offers innovative tips and tricks as well as savvy advice that will save you time and increase your productivity.

Available wherever books are sold.

WILEY
Now you know.